FOLLOW THOSE WOMEN

Church Women in the Ecumenical Movement

A History of the Development of United Work Among Women of the
Protestant Churches in the United States

GLADYS GILKEY CALKINS

Library of Congress Catalog Card Number: 61-17252

Published for United Church Women
NATIONAL COUNCIL OF THE CHURCHES OF CHRIST IN U.S.A.
by the Office of Publication and Distribution
475 Riverside Drive, New York 27, New York
$1.25

F 01-58   Copyright © 1961, National Council of Churches   Printed in U.S.A.

CONTENTS

INTRODUCTION

Tʜᴇ ɪᴅᴇᴀ which led in 1941 to the founding of the United Council of Church Women and brought this organization, in 1950, into the newly-formed National Council of the Churches of Christ in the United States of America as the "General Department of United Church Women" was an idea which already had behind it the development of more than half a century. Its future is still in the making.

Behind these fifty years, of course, lies the whole long story of the relation of women to the Christian Church. Women have always been a recognized part of the Body of Christ, deeply committed to its faith and loyal in its service to the limit of their capacities and opportunities. But the tremendous changes of the last century brought changes in the form and expression of that relationship, especially in America. Here the doors that opened to women in the years after the Civil War to higher education and to fuller participation in every phase of American society awakened in them at the same time a great desire to share more fully and more effectively in the life of the Church.

This history attempts to trace not the entire story of the latter but one important part of it: the development of united work among women in the Protestant churches.

1

It is a story worth telling both because it is a valid part of the history of Protestantism in America which has so far received scant attention at the hands of church historians, and because, in the course of it, women as a group have found a way to make contributions characteristically their own to the life of the Church in this country. Why organization was necessary for this will perhaps appear. Our story deals more specifically with national than with local developments, and with united rather than denominational interests, though, as we shall see, these facets merge one into the other.

THE idea of united work among the women of the churches has had from the beginning elements of both dream and conviction. Dream it was, because at every step its achievement was beset by practical difficulties and its actual fulfillment seemed highly unlikely. Yet all the time women felt sure they were being led in this direction. Like Abraham they did not know the details of the country toward which they felt called to travel, but they walked on by faith, ready to do what seemed right as this appeared.

At the same time it was a conviction. They felt increasingly sure that uniting of their forces in *some* form was a necessity, if they were ever to accomplish the things that seemed to them important to be done. Church institutions, local and national, were strongholds of conservatism in regard to the participation of women. As individuals, women felt at a disadvantage in a church world presided over by clerics and lay men. They needed the confidence and the experience that action as a group supplied.

But this sense of the necessity of "unitedness" did not keep women from being loyal to the individual church and the denominational communion in whose tradition they were reared. The apparent paradox involved in this has been the occasion of some misunderstanding and some criticism of the existence of a separate organization of women within the churches. History, however, shows that any conflict in women's loyalty at this point has been more apparent than real. Moreover, again and again it has been the women most active in denominational affairs who have been most interested in the development of united work.

But it was never a cramped or narrow denominationalism which such women supported. Their loyalty to the larger conception was strengthened rather than undercut by the conviction (or intuition, if you will) that the Church as the Body of Christ was the richer for the gifts that all groups within it, including women, could bring to it. Unity can be seen in the light of particularity. Neither need destroy the other.

This paradox must be understood and granted if one is rightly to appraise the significance of united work among church women. It is best interpreted perhaps by saying there has always been a wider dimension to their dream of "unitedness" than any organizational goal for themselves. The fellowship of work and worship fostered among women in the Protestant churches beginning early in the twentieth century was a dynamic, meaningful experience that was ecumenical in nature. No church woman who was in sympathy with its objectives was excluded from participation. Its approach was apt to be practical rather than theological. But the principle underlying organized united work was the same as that which found expression in the utterances of the great ecumenical conferences of Oxford and Edinburgh in 1937, and was embodied in the plans for a World Council of Churches in 1948. By 1937, this women's movement had been in existence for many years. Here was a contribution to the early growth and spread of the ecumenical movement in the American churches which has not always been recognized.

Women seem to have been influenced always by the ideal of the essential oneness of God's people and his kingdom, and hence were concerned for the united task of the Christian

Church. In the nineteenth century this led them to support interdenominational efforts of all kinds, and was certainly one of their motives in creating women's interdenominational mission boards and councils. In the twentieth century it led them to experiment not only with united (as distinct from interdenominational) work, but with various kinds of co-operative effort with other religious bodies. It led them finally to accept incorporation in the new National Council of the Churches of Christ in the U.S.A. in 1950, even though this meant a certain loss in the very identity that they had struggled so hard to achieve.

At the moment of critical decision, when a choice had to be made, it was the larger vision of the oneness of the total Christian Church and not the smaller dream of women's unity in that endeavor that triumphed. The lesser loyalty was kept, but subordinated. In the long look of history this, too, may have been a contribution of church women to an understanding of the ultimate choice entailed by the Christian conception of the Church.

CHAPTER 1

Rooted in Missions
1865-1920

The movement that drew Protestant women together nationally after World War I had roots which reach far back into the nineteenth century. These are important because they reveal as nothing else could the reasons for the development of united work, and the character of its early program.

The decades following the Civil War were stirring ones. Prosperity had returned at least in the North and Midwest; changes were in the air. Population, especially in the cities, was growing rapidly, industries were starting, immigrants were arriving, business was booming.

As far as women were concerned, they were more in evidence than in the ante-bellum days, but it was still without question a man's world. The movement to obtain political suffrage had begun in 1848, but it would be years before it would be granted. But suffrage was only one aspect of what has been called the "woman movement." In all areas women were beginning to reach out to play a fuller part in the life of the day. This included higher education, the professions, industry, business, and a growing number of voluntary activities outside their homes. Traditions and customs never before questioned were being challenged.

The attitude of the churches toward the place of women

5

was a conservative one. Women had no official status in them except as members of the congregation. But changes had been coming indirectly. Since the beginning of the century, women had been meeting in organized groups for the support and study of missions, a work of Christian witness and enlightenment in which they deeply believed. The very names of these early groups suggest the limitations that surrounded their efforts: "Female Mite Society," the "Pious Female Praying Society," the "Cent Society." After the Civil War a few brave spirits gathered groups of church women around them and braved public opinion by starting humanitarian projects in the community to meet the needs of the poverty stricken or of the women working in the new factories. Among these were the early Young Women's Christian Associations. Women's area of experience was slowly widening and organization was no longer a novelty.

Women's interest in the missionary opportunities open to the Church increased as they saw for themselves the needs of immigrant families, heard of the dearth of the gospel in the Far West as the moving frontier opened for settlement, and listened to the appeals of missionaries returning from foreign lands. They had little money of their own to give but they were deeply concerned and determined to do what they could. They continued to save offerings for home and foreign missions from butter and egg money, or baked pies and cookies to sell. They pieced innumerable quilts and made rags into carpets in order to earn something to give for the promotion of the gospel.

There is no evidence that women helped to administer the money they raised. It was turned over to the general boards of the denominations whose male members then allocated it to benevolent and mission work. Even so, the early societies had to face suspicion instead of encouragement from the local clergy. When asked about his women's society one clergyman wrote that he made it a point to attend women's missionary prayer meetings "because you never could tell what women might take to praying about if left alone."*

The idea that single women as well as men with wives could be useful on the mission field had been suggested as early as 1835 by returning missionaries who realized that women and children in the Orient had special needs that women might serve even better than men. But the idea was so bitterly opposed by the denominational boards that it was dropped. It was considered quite improper to send single women; only if husbands could be found before sailing could they go. But the boards were generous, and on occasion even offered to secure the husbands!

In 1861, a group of missionary-minded women, under the leadership of Mrs. Thomas Doremus, determined to do something about this. In New York City a "Union Missionary Society" was formed for the express purpose of promoting the sending out of women missionaries. It was in fact the first interdenominational society of which we have record, though this seems to have been incidental. Its immediate objective was to meet the need for special work among women and children on the mission field, now even more apparent than before. The new society communicated its conviction and its vision of the possibilities to others, and succeeded in raising the unheard of sum of two thousand dollars.

We hear little further of this first union society. Its unique beginning seems not to have led to other interdenominational efforts, but rather to the securing of separate women's boards of missions within the various denominations. The appearance of these was undoubtedly a stimulus to generally increased missionary activity, and by the women was considered a real step forward. They felt that at last the special interests of women in relation to

---

* From "Recollections of Mrs. Thomas Doremus," published in a newspaper dated 1910.

the missionary enterprise would be more adequately taken into account. It was a satisfaction, too, that the financing of the projects for which they raised special funds would no longer be under the control of the men's boards.

In the next two decades women's boards were organized in nearly every Protestant denomination. The Women's Foreign Missionary Society of The Methodist Church dates from 1869; the same year it sent Miss Isabella Thoburn to India and appointed Miss Clara Swain as a medical missionary. These had the distinction of being the first missionaries sent by a women's board to the foreign field. In 1870, the Women's Foreign Missionary Society of the Presbyterian Church USA sent a woman missionary to China, and the United Presbyterian Women, one to Africa. The women of the Disciples of Christ formed a board of missions in 1873, which sent both men and women to home and foreign fields.

Church membership grew from 16 to 36 per cent of the population between 1850 and 1890, and the increased prosperity of the churches helped undoubtedly to make all these developments possible. Women's boards not only pioneered in new projects but were able to raise the funds to support them.

In 1890 and 1891, a large interdenominational committee of women from these various boards was formed to help put on a program for the World's Fair in Chicago in 1893, and in 1900, the denominational women's boards helped in the preparation for the great Ecumenical Conference on Foreign Missions in New York.

It was an age characterized inside and outside the church world by large organizations and expansive plans. The YMCA was spreading rapidly. New lay organizations appeared, such as the Society for Christian Endeavor (1881) and the Student Volunteer Movement (1886). The Foreign Missions Conference of North America was founded in 1894. The World Evangelical Alliance came to this country in 1893, and the World Student Christian Federation, a vision of John R. Mott, dates from 1894.

Enthusiasm for Christian missions mounted in the churches. It reached its peak in the Laymen's Missionary Movement of 1905 and similar "forward movements." At the same time voices critical of conditions in American society had become increasingly insistent. By the turn of the century the Social Gospel, to which many in the churches had at first been hostile, was making an increasing impact on the thinking of men and women members. The strikes of the eighteen-nineties had been ominous and social reform was overdue. The ideas of men like Washington Gladden and Walter Rauschenbusch were bearing fruit, and the latter's book, *Christianity and the Social Crisis,* published in 1907, was widely read and made a profound impression. The Federal Council of Churches, with its controversial "Social Creed of the Churches," came into existence in 1908.

THE contribution of church women to this change of attitude has not always been recognized. Home missions had given many of them some idea of the poverty and misery that prevailed in "foreign" sections of the cities. The plight of children and the unfulfilled hopes of the immigrants crowding through Ellis Island to a land of promise roused their sympathies and would not let them be complacent. Not being immediately involved in the bitter controversies of the times, they were freer to see the terrible cost in human lives of unlimited competition and the assumptions of the "gospel of wealth." They were disposed to be more liberal than their husbands even on such issues as protective legislation and the right of workers to organize in their own behalf. Within the Church their opinion was not often expressed or asked, but women furnished a substantial body of support for the more socially liberal point of view.

In regard to the international scene church women had

learned most of what they knew about foreign lands and their cultures from mission maps and stories. The motto of the Student Volunteer Movement, "The evangelization of the world in this generation," did not seem at all impossible, and they were ready to believe in a Christian "manifest destiny" for America. They shared the buoyantly hopeful mood of the country in these years when good causes of all kinds abounded and the future was unclouded.

Yet even in these years of general optimism, women were not content with generalities. Part of their natural endowment seems always to have been a gift for finding and diligently pursuing concrete ways of working toward ideal goals. A number of imaginative experiments started during this period proved to have lasting value.

In 1887, Mrs. Darwin R. James, then president of the Woman's Board of Home Missions of the Presbyterian Church USA, suggested to her local societies that church women be urged to meet together on a specific day in their own communities to pray for the cause of home missions. Women responded with so much interest that such a day continued to be set apart annually and other denominations soon joined in the plan. In 1890, Mrs. Henry Peabody and Mrs. Helen Barrett Montgomery, both prominent in the Baptist denomination, suggested a similar Day of Prayer for foreign missions. This, too, caught the imagination and spread rapidly. The idea of special days of united prayer was destined to play an important part from this time on in developing a sense of unity and common purpose among all Christian women.

Another experiment of permanent value had to do with the joint production and promotion of better material as a basis for missionary study. The great ecumenical World Missionary Conference held in New York in 1900 proved to be a stirring experience, and the denominational women who attended it conceived the idea of uniting for the very practical purpose of stimulating an interest in missions through producing reliable information about it and by promoting mission study. All denominations would use this study material. This eminently sensible idea resulted in the first truly interdenominational undertaking by the women's boards of missions. A "Central Committee on the United Study of Foreign Missions" was set up in 1901 and two years later a similar one for home missions. The two eventually united. For thirty years, until 1938 when its work was turned over to the Missionary Education Movement, this Central Committee performed a function of great usefulness. It insisted that manuscripts be of high quality, and was itself responsible for editing, publishing, and widely promoting their use. This work not only raised the level of missionary literature, but did much to co-ordinate the missionary interests of all the church groups.

It also led quite naturally to another kind of united activity—the holding of area and regional schools of missions in the summer. The first of these was held in 1907 in the Midwest, at Winona Lake, Indiana. Others in the East, at Silver Bay, New York, and Northfield, Massachusetts, followed soon. They were very popular during the next decades and became established institutions, attracting outstanding women for their leadership. Women enjoyed the experience of leaving their families for a week to be in a pleasant spot under the inspiration of good speakers, for a combination of serious study and mild recreation. By 1920, twelve such interdenominational schools were in operation in as many regions continuing to foster a spirit of fellowship between church women.

Another project of practical usefulness was developed in 1914 to provide women and children in China, India, Korea, and Japan, who had recently learned to read, with the kind of simple reading material which did not exist and was greatly needed. A Committee on Christian Literature for Women and Children was organized; supported by gifts from the mission boards and individuals, it was responsible for the production of magazines, leaflets, books, and illustrated material in various languages. Its work still continues with a sum of $45,000 appropriated annually for this purpose from the World Day of Prayer offerings.

It was the enthusiasm engendered by the successful work of the Central Committee that led in 1911 to the planning of a series of Jubilee meetings across the country, to celebrate the fifty years of denominational women's work for foreign missions (1860-1910). The Edinburgh World Missionary Conference had just taken place, and preparation for this Jubilee followed its pattern of careful planning. Mrs. Helen Barrett Montgomery of Rochester and Mrs. Henry Peabody of Boston were appointed to head up the meetings. Mrs. Montgomery was a New Testament scholar and a writer as well. Her book, *Western Women in Eastern Lands,* had been the 1910 study book published by the Central Committee. Now she wrote and produced a pageant for the Jubilee in which two hundred women took part.

Both Mrs. Montgomery and Mrs. Peabody were dynamic speakers. They presented missions not as a by-product or side-issue of Christianity, but as its very essence and its central challenge. The opportunity to have a part in this great enterprise was open to every woman in the church. The call was for numbers, not just for the small groups in the traditional missionary society. Women were aroused by this direct appeal. They arranged innumerable public meetings which attracted large audiences, and they opened their homes for the new and popular "drawing-room meetings" for smaller groups.

It was suggested that American women raise a Jubilee fund of one million dollars as a united gift to their Lord for use in the spreading of his kingdom. The success of the meetings and of this effort led to the founding of the Federation of Women's Boards of Foreign Missions to help administer these funds co-operatively. The Council of Women for Home Missions had already been organized in 1908. Women, too, in order to work effectively, were constrained to follow the general trend toward consolidation and large organization.

THE Jubilee event contributed greatly to the development of local interdenominational missionary groups. Records show that some united women's groups had been organized much earlier. The Woman's Missionary Union of Springfield, Missouri, for example, dates from 1887, when its constitution was adopted at an "all-day missionary meeting" which three hundred women from eleven churches attended. The Missionary Social Union of St. Louis dates from 1898; the Missionary Federation of Kansas City from 1909. After 1911, the number of such groups rapidly increased.

The Jubilee meetings had been a glorious experience locally of a new kind of fellowship in a great cause—across denominational lines. To perpetuate this seemed so natural that its significance was not immediately comprehended. But it was, in fact, a departure from past practice. It is true that at the national top of the church structure, missionary boards had some time before adopted the interdenominational pattern of working together. But in local communities the invisible walls that separated the work, as well as the worship, of Presbyterians, Baptists, Methodists and others were still high. In many a community the Jubilee meetings had broken through those walls and women in the Protestant communions had found each other.

They liked what they had found and intended to keep it. Follow-up meetings were held which led to the next step—some continuing form of organization. An interdenominational group was organized in Buffalo, New York, that same year, giving as its motive one that must have been typical of the many united groups that came into existence shortly after 1911: "The Buffalo Jubilee was indeed a mountain-top experience, and it was then that women in our churches learned the joy of working together."*

The names adopted by these groups were many and varied. "Missionary Unions," "Missionary Federations," "Councils of Missions" predominated. For lack of a common name we shall refer to them as local united groups. Their central interest was the study and promotion of home and foreign missions and for this purpose the study books published by the Central Committee lay ready at hand. The days of prayer, already become a tradition, became naturally the two foci of their year's calendar. The Day of Prayer for Foreign Missions came during "foreign missions week" in January, and for Home Missions during "home mission week" in November. It is important to remember that women in the united groups cut no ties with their own churches or denominational missionary societies but remained loyal members of both.

Wherever local federations of churches existed, as they did in some of the larger cities at this time, women's groups either affiliated or co-operated with them. But membership in the women's united groups was never linked directly with denominational representation. Vice-presidents were, as a rule, representative of the various churches, but membership from the beginning seems to have been a matter of personal commitment to the purpose of the group. All church women were eligible. Here was the germ of a different basis for coming together than that of a strictly interdenominational structure. It was one that was to grow in significance.

Women found in these new groups a wider freedom in determining policy and program than they had known before. They were free from clerical and male control in this regard, though they often asked advice. They looked for guidance nationally to the women's missionary boards, but

* "History of United Church Women of Buffalo and Vicinity," written to commemorate their Fiftieth Anniversary, 1961.

technically were free to engage in activities other than missions if they wished. It was an intangible freedom but real enough to women who had not experienced it before within their own churches. It was not long before the results of this opportunity to exercise leadership began to be apparent in the development of women leaders who could carry responsibility and grow in the capacity to do so in the group and in the community.

For all these reasons the number of women's united groups grew rapidly after 1911. Some remained content with a program of mission study and with the observance of the days of prayer. But others developed a strong organization and began to branch out into a more varied program which often included special projects of a humanitarian nature in the community. When war broke on the American scene in 1917, many of them were able to contribute constructively to special wartime needs in the community, but the records of such activities are hidden in the histories of local groups.

In an age which put a premium upon bigness and tended to equate size with success, women were a stabilizing influence wherever they found an opportunity to function in Church or society, because they had a different standard of measurement. If a project served the needs of people, it was worth attempting. Taught by long experience not to underestimate small things, women were not discouraged by small meetings, small support, small funds. They seem to have taken permanently to heart the advice of a sympathetic pastor, who in the early days had opened his church to a group seeking to organize. The day was very stormy and four women arrived. "Organize," he counseled them. "Go ahead just as though the room were full."*

"Fear not, little flock . . ." was a passage of Scripture whose meaning these women understood. That so much

---

* *Forward Together,* by Mabel Head. United Council of Church Women, New York, 1950.

could be accomplished by so few, with such limited resources, was a constant miracle which only the promise of the Lord to his "little flock" could explain. If women were unsuccessful in a given effort, they were not surprised. If successful, they were not disposed to give undue credit to any special wisdom or technique. But they took heart from small achievements. Modest in their expectations, they kept on persistently, unafraid.

These were qualities which would stand church women in good stead in the two decades of disillusionment and depression which followed the close of World War I.

CHAPTER 2

Decade of Development
1919-1929

WORLD WAR I had the effect of ringing down a sudden curtain on the idealism and unlimited optimism character-istic of pre-war America. Americans had worked earnestly for peace, and were shocked when the war they had thought impossible engulfed Europe in 1914. They were still un-prepared when neutrality broke down and America found herself in 1917 a reluctant partner in the conflict. Once the country was involved, however, public opinion changed al-most overnight. The reasons back of this were themselves idealistic. Was this not to be the "war to end war," one that would make the "world safe for democracy"? Churches joined wholeheartedly in promoting Liberty Bond sales while women knitted sweaters and socks at their meetings.

Measured against these high expectations, however, the results of the war were disappointing. The fervor with which America had fought gave way in 1918 to a general desire to retreat from international involvement that prom-ised to be difficult rather than glorious. President Wilson's idea of maintaining peace through a League of Nations was overwhelmingly rejected. This swing to isolation and reac-tion was accentuated by the fact that, after a brief reces-sion in 1920, prosperity returned and good times in Amer-ica were better than ever. Interest in idealistic enterprises of all kinds definitely declined. The InterChurch World Movement, which had launched a great campaign at the close of the war in the hope of achieving a federation of the evangelical churches for charitable and religious purposes supported by large funds, wholly failed to find a response. The public was not interested in such enterprises and preferred to turn its attention to other matters.

Social reform, too, seemed to have had its day. Few voices spoke out either from the pulpit or in the secular press to disturb the general mood of preoccupation and ease. Commercial entertainment of all kinds was making a successful bid for the national attention, and it was estimated that fifty million Americans every week attended the new moving picture theatres that appeared in every community. The Ford car made its appearance at a price that most people could afford. Habits of recreation were changing. It was the age of "speak-easies" and taverns, dance halls and beauty contests. There was much to make the socially-minded uneasy. Fundamentalism had gathered its forces to attack religious liberalism, not only in its theological aspects but in its social outlook.

Church women in the local united groups were a part of this post-war America, influenced by all the factors in it that were unpromising for their objectives. Could they be expected to accomplish much during a period of disillusionment and retreat? Without status in the church world, without experienced leadership or funds, they might be forgiven if they conducted only a holding operation during a period peculiarly indifferent to their aims.

But the contrary was true. The earliest reliable figures date from 1924, when the Federal Council of Churches made a survey and found 1,200 united groups in existence. A decade later the number was carefully checked again and more than 1,900 were reported. Most of them were without organized program and some met only once or twice a year, but numerically, at least, they were growing in number. The nineteen-twenties witnessed an extension of the Day of Prayer observance now linked with the support of women's missionary projects, increasing social concern among many of the stronger groups, and the first attempts to bring about some form of united organization nationally.

Perhaps the right of political suffrage newly given to them in 1920 spurred women to feel a special sense of civic responsibility. In any case they were sensitive to moral values and worried about the effect of post-war standards on their children and their families. Much needed to be done to meet new needs that were appearing. Laws needed to be enforced, moving pictures needed to be improved, women and children in industry needed protection. The fact that in the churches as a whole there was little interest in the Social Gospel in the nineteen-twenties did not particularly affect women's concern about these questions. Their approach to social issues was essentially pragmatic and not doctrinaire. Women were concerned about the welfare and needs of individuals; while this had made them sympathetic to the preaching of the Social Gospel, it had not left them dependent upon it. To try to bring a more abundant life to women and children in foreign lands, and to do what was needed in this country and in the community, was still their motive and purpose. The battle of Fundamentalism versus Liberalism might rage in the pulpits, and the Scopes trial make headlines in the newspapers, but these would not throw the women off course. There was too much that needed to be done.

For the same reason it can be readily understood why women's belief in prayer was never incompatible with their support of missionary projects of a very practical nature. Schools, hospitals and equipment supplied, rather, the *subjects* for prayer. These were wonderful ways by which the more abundant life could be made more of a reality for God's children.

In 1921, as a united project, the church women of America raised over two million dollars, mostly in very small amounts, to provide greatly needed housing facilities and staff for Christian colleges for women in the Orient. The story is told of a little boy who rang his neighbor's doorbell during the campaign and held out his box saying, "Please, will you help me? I've got to raise a million dollars to build a college in China." Whether apocryphal or not, the story illustrates the spirit of those who made a success of the effort. It was an amazing achievement, a compound of concern, hard work, and much prayer. The two million was augmented by a third million from the Laura Spelman Rockefeller Fund, and made possible several new women's colleges overseas.

Concrete projects of this kind became related to the Day of Prayer for Missions as yearly objects of special support and intercession. In 1919, as a result of requests from local groups, the days of prayer for home and foreign missions had been combined, with the first Friday in Lent chosen for the observance. Canadian women asked to participate in 1920, and from this year on, the idea of a united Day of Prayer for all church women spread rapidly. Missionaries carried it back with them to their stations abroad. It was received with enthusiasm in Europe as well as in Asia, in Africa, and in the islands of the Pacific. It was a wholly natural development that in 1927 it became in name, as it had already in fact, a "World Day of Prayer for Missions." Before the term ecumenical came into common use, the World Day of Prayer had this connotation. It was the symbol, dynamic and deeply cherished, of the common faith and the common task that unites in one bond all women who profess to follow Christ, whatever their race, creed, or nation.

The first offering in 1920 had been entirely spontaneous, amounting to $70. By 1926, so large an offering was coming in from Day of Prayer observances and being conscientiously and equally divided between the foreign and home mission boards, that allocations from it were becoming an important source of support for interdenominational projects. In this year a special allocation was set aside for Christian Literature for Women and Children in Mission Lands. Work among sharecroppers and migrant agricultural workers in America, support of religious workers in American Indian schools, the continuing support of women's Christian colleges in the Orient became special projects of the Day.

There is no way of knowing how many women took part in the first united observance in 1920, but we do know that they used 50,000 copies of a prepared program, and that the materials related to the Day increased every year. By 1930, the offering had increased, in spite of the advent of depression, to $20,000.

The Parable of the Mustard Seed was a reality to these women, as they measured their gifts and efforts against the limitless needs and equally limitless possibilities represented by the projects which they had now adopted as specifically theirs. Awareness of this forever kept them from forgetting their dependence upon a power greater than their own.

Efforts of church women in the social field were modest and experimental in comparison with well-established programs such as those of the YWCA and social service agencies, but they show a concern to interpret responsible citizenship as a part of Christian commitment.

Their zeal helped direct attention to problems in the community and helped arouse church people to the needs of the community. A local group was organized in Rochester, New York, in 1922, which wrote this purpose into its constitution: "To unify the women of the churches for Christian civic and social endeavor by the exchange of experiences and inspiration . . . and to promote the functioning of organized women's work with the social agencies."*

* "History of the Council of Church Women of Rochester and Vicinity," 1957.

The first departments which it set up in addition to Missions were a Community Service Department, Young People's Department, and an Americanization Committee. Later, such activities as a Volunteer Motor Service, a Christmas Bureau, and a Volunteer Department for the Council of Social Agencies were added.

Some projects were not without a humorous aspect. The San Diego union recommended that church women in that city work for "a new jail, improvement in Children's and Tubercular Wards and the installation of a Rock Pile for drunken drivers." It recorded earlier that the group had not only helped with plans for a Chinese church and a dormitory for young Chinese men but a general "day of Abstinence" had been tried. The latter was not successful, however, ". . . because delicate and elderly ladies could not endure the fast."*

It is not strange that women who had found meaning and strength in praying together, also found that they could usefully work together as Christians on all kinds of unmet needs in the community. But the problem this posed of supplying standards and helpful guidance for these burgeoning programs will be readily understood. The national bodies to which the local groups still looked were the Federation of Women's Boards of Foreign Missions and the Council of Women for Home Missions. The whole question of the kind of activities outside the field of missions, that were appropriate for local groups, worried them. As early as 1918, a joint meeting of a Committee on Conference of the two bodies had recorded "calls from interdenominational missionary unions for some program of service that might be prepared for them by the Federation and Council." That they were thinking mainly in denominational terms is indicated by their conclusion that there was "need for a local organization which should, by comparison of

---

* "Milestones and Reflections Through Three Decades, 1926-1956," History of United Church Women of San Diego.

methods and new enthusiasm, stimulate all to greater effort in their denominational work."

The boards set themselves to help as well as they could, though they were not set up organizationally to do so. They appointed a "Joint Committee on Women's Church and Missionary Federations" which prepared a suggested constitution for them and a leaflet dealing with local program and objectives.

The Federal Council of Churches looked with some concern on the growing independence of such groups. At the close of World War I, there were strong and active federations in many of the larger cities, but the Federal Council had on the whole been less successful than it had hoped to be in promoting interdenominational organization of such federations on a country-wide basis. Nothing in their constitutions excluded women, and, as a matter of fact, some women had served on their national committees and administrative board almost from the beginning. In some cities the local federation of churches had taken the initiative in helping groups of church women to organize under their sponsorship. Should these not logically remain an integral part of the federation structure locally, where they could add strength to an interdenominational co-operative effort already under way?

In 1921, a survey was made under the auspices of the Federal Council to see what place women actually had in local church federations, and what societies of women were doing. It seems to have been the first survey of the role of women in the Church. Two states and twenty-four cities replied to the questionnaire. The reports were revealing not only of the situation but of the climate of opinion and custom that produced it. No reply indicated that women in the churches could not be elected to church boards and committees, or as official representatives to local federations or other bodies, but eight said they never had been. Eight others said that few women were used. Six reported women's united organizations in existence. Reports showed that church women were engaged in church visitations, social service, survey of motion pictures, raising money, and social action in the community. But most of the secretaries who submitted them thought that the organization of women's groups was neither essential nor advisable.

When the survey came up for discussion, the following policy was adopted:

1. Where church federations or councils exist, each member church shall be represented by the pastor, a layman, and a laywoman, the last named to be chosen by the combined vote of the women's missionary organizations of the church.

2. That there shall be an autonomous department made up of women members which shall be related to the Federation of Women's Boards of Foreign Missions and the Council of Women for Home Missions, organized according to their suggested constitution. This department shall have full charge of interdenominational study work, inspirational meetings and so forth, as outlined by the federation and council.

3. Where no church federation or council exists, the women shall be encouraged to organize as noted in 2, and hold themselves ready to affiliate when a federation or council of churches comes into existence.

Although the first point represented a distinct gain in recommending that women be appointed as church representatives, the report did not solve the future of women's united groups.

These provisions continued to be the official policy of the Federal Council for some years, and many women's groups tried with more or less success to fit into the existing structure. They were never wholly satisfactory, and so did not solve the question of relationship permanently. The assumptions of equality that seemed to underlie the recommendations had no real basis, and the timing of them as a reform policy was both too late and too soon. It was too late, in that women had already worked out a more satisfying pattern of operation than that offered by polite inclusion in the federation structure without real participation in its policies and plans. The disposition of the funds they themselves had raised was a delicate matter, when over-all policy was still in general practice a male prerogative. It was too early, in that women still lacked in experience and self-assurance. They were more at ease in their own separate organizations.

At the same time church women did not want to appear disloyal to existing organizations, especially those which were promoting church co-operation. They had no desire to be "irregular." They were quite willing to acknowledge the authority and experience of the Federal Council in interdenominational matters and in its social program, and to turn to it for help and guidance in unifying their own efforts, even if they were not ready to identify with it completely in organization.

In October, 1924, the executive secretary of the Committee on Local Federations and Councils of the Federal Council asked for a conference with the president of the Women's Boards of Foreign Missions and of the Council of Women for Home Missions on the whole question of local united women's groups. He reported that on going through the council's files he had found a great many letters from various women's interdenominational church groups. All of them "expressed the desire that the Federal Council would take the initiative in bringing into existence a national organization which would provide the logical integrating medium of communication and co-operation for the state and local interdenominational groups of church women then existing."

The two presidents, Mrs. E. H. Silverthorn of New York and Mrs. John Ferguson, presently of California, were national Presbyterian leaders who were sympathetic to local problems. They sensed that the moment was auspicious for some new action that might lead forward and lent their support. As a result of this interview, the Federal Council issued an invitation to the two mission bodies to have their representatives meet with others from the Association of Council Secretaries of state and local federations and councils, and from local women's groups, in Pittsburgh, on December 11 and 12, 1924, to consider a unified approach in communities, and possible co-ordination of group activities.

The meeting was held with an officer of the Federal Council presiding. Statements of fact and opinion were made by many of the secretaries which are quoted at length in the minutes. There is no indication that statements were asked from any of the women. But women were present and they did take part in the discussion that followed. Recommendations resulted that urged a greater flexibility in missionary programs and a study of the work of nonchurch agencies in the community. But more important for the future was the suggestion that the same five participating agencies plan to meet again and annually, for further discussions.

Such conferences did in fact take place for the next five years and marked a year-by-year development. It was becoming increasingly evident that the two interdenominational mission bodies, organized as they were functionally to perform certain services, were not prepared to assume full responsibility for such widely inclusive programs as were developing in the local groups. It would have required more internal adjustments in their work than the denominational mission boards felt it was fitting for them to make, even though they were sympathetic and co-operative. Some of their members were among the most active supporters of the new development.

It was also evident that women would not for long depend upon Federal Council initiative. At the second annual meeting, held in Cleveland, June, 1926, a clergyman presided again, but a woman, Mrs. Silverthorn, functioned as the chairman of the program committee, and herself led a symposium on "Co-operative Organized Work." At the third conference, held in St. Louis in 1927, a woman, Mrs. John Ferguson, the able president of the Council of Women for Home Missions, presided. After 1927, the men from the Federal Council seem to have dropped out of the picture, except as they functioned in some advisory capacity.

IT was in this same year that women published their own first study of the place of women in the life of the Church. This was called, significantly, the "Relative Place of Women in the Church," and brought up the question "whether in the light of a larger release of their powers elsewhere in life, there needed to be a revision of the dimensions of their sphere in the Church." Directed by Miss Clarissa Spencer and Miss Elizabeth Wilson of the staff of the National Board, YWCA, it was carefully prepared. The appendix, tabulating replies received from 114 denominations, was the first compilation of facts regarding the actual status of women in contemporary American church life. The report discussed tendencies that were hopeful, and changes needed. Among the "tendencies," the report notes: ". . . a tendency to cease to contemplate the peculiar contribution which women can make to the Church because the characteristics generally cited are possessed by both men and women"; and a "trend to forget sex and make the person the basis of selection." It ended with a suggestion, wholly in the realm of prophecy in 1927, that ". . . the whole work of the Church should be planned by men and women working together."

At the Cleveland, 1926, Conference the following activities were suggested as appropriate for local groups: (1) A comprehensive educational program covering the Day of Prayer for Missions. (2) Institutes on Mission Study, Social Service, Religious Education, International Relations and World Peace, and Law Observance. The following year the St. Louis Conference added Christian Citizenship, Industrial and Race Relations to the list, indicating how rapidly the social concerns of local groups were increasing. One statement from a later account of the St. Louis proceedings sums up this development:

"Church agencies are not static; the same broadening of interest that has come to women generally has touched the women's missionary organizations of the churches, and has been reflected in the topics forming part of their program. . . . Christian citizenship and these other interests are not denominational tasks but are common to all Christian women."

It was from this same Conference of 1927 that there came the first definite expression of desire for a central organization that would correlate the work of the local groups. Neither the national home and foreign mission bodies nor the Federal Council had proved to be the right foster parents for them permanently. They must, they felt, create a family of their own to which to belong. "The coming together in conference for three successive years has revealed the fact that church women throughout America are recognizing the need for an interdenominational national organization through which the work of local interdenominational groups of church women may be correlated, systematized and promoted."*

In the months after the St. Louis Conference, an almost unbelievable number of discussions and conferences on this problem took place. We need not follow them in detail. There was much conscientious wrestling with the question of right relationships, particularly with the two mission bodies. If the question seems to us unnecessarily labored and the process confused, we must remember not only the missionary roots from which the groups had sprung but the fact that missions and the World Day of Prayer were still

---

* Report of St. Louis Conference, June, 1927.

the major interest of the majority. For more than fifty years, moreover, mission boards had been the only national organizations of church women. Women did not want to seem disloyal, or be misunderstood by these organizations to which, in the Church, they had owed so much. Women were no less devoted to missions now than in the past. But opportunity and need in the community had changed with the years, and something new was called for to enlist women whose capacities for leadership and service had also changed. The leaders of the new movement hoped to avoid possible difficulties by being meticulous. They were more anxious to move carefully than to move swiftly. A Committee on Conference was set up which was representative of all the national bodies whose interests were involved.

Mrs. John Ferguson, who had been so intimately connected with the new movement, was elected chairman of this committee. At an important meeting in December, 1927, she presented a careful historical resumé which has been preserved for us. At the close of the frank discussion that followed, the representatives of the seven major interdenominational organizations present approved, in principle, the idea that some kind of central organization of church women should be permitted. But it was agreed that there should be some kind of guiding group from the mission bodies as advisors "to insure a proper continued attention to missionary interests."

At the next annual Conference which met in Buffalo, New York, on May 30, 1928, this "Guiding Group" was formally constituted and its duties outlined: to plan for local interdenominational church women's groups; unify and enlarge their programs; counsel and advise new organizations; co-operate with the Federal Council of Churches and the Association of Council Secretaries. With so many important responsibilities on its shoulders, a more adequate name than "Guiding Group" seemed indicated. The following day a new name was adopted, the "National Commission of

Protestant Church Women," and the commission proceded to elect Mrs. John Ferguson as chairman and Mrs. E. H. Silverthorn, vice-chairman.

The newly appointed executive was Mrs. Josephine M. Stearns of Indianapolis, an active Disciple leader. Describing the general feeling that something of unusual importance for the future had taken place at this business session, she wrote: "At last the link has been forged which binds together Christian women of America, enabling them to speak with one voice, to have comradeship in service, to federate their activities and enjoy the interchange of plans and methods."*

Not all the items on the agenda of the Buffalo Conference were organizational, however. The keynote address of the conference had been given by Mrs. Silverthorn, who had just returned from the history-making World Conference on Missions in Jerusalem. Her message communicated the vision she had received at Jerusalem of the Church Universal, whose great purpose it must be to do God's will by witnessing to his rule in every area of human life, as well as to the ends of the earth. Women were deeply moved by her words and saw in them the expression of their own earnest hopes and motives in organizing the National Commission of Protestant Women.

Before the final session of the new National Commission on June 2, 1928, plans were laid for moving forward into the new opportunities that lay open before the women. Sincere prayers of gratitude for all that had been accomplished, and earnest ones for guidance closed a meeting which was felt to be an answer to prayer. Almost immediately there were evidences that the forming of the National Commission of Protestant Church Women was significant not only to the group that had worked so long for it but to the country at large. The Associated Press

---

* Quoted in Historical Sketch by Mrs. John Ferguson, reprinted in *News Bulletin,* November, 1936.

gave the event ample coverage, and in the New York *Times* it was front page news.

"A unique and unprecedented meeting was held in Buffalo, June 1. Fewer than 50 women were present but they were delegated representatives who came together to consummate plans for the bringing into existence of a Federation of Protestant Church Women of America. This new organization is called 'The National Commission of Protestant Church Women.' "*

An office was opened at 1123 Broadway in New York City. Expressions of interest poured in. A church woman from St. Louis sent in a gift of $500, a godsend to an organization which had started with completely empty coffers! By agreement with the Federation of Women's Boards of Foreign Missions and the Council of Women for Home Missions, local groups had been released from the payment of the customary membership dues to these national bodies in order to support the Commission. It was hoped that local dues and contributions to the new National Commission would meet the anticipated budget of $9,000.

The address at 1123 Broadway, New York City, became widely known in the country and even abroad. Mrs. Ferguson made a visit to South America and had an opportunity to confer with church women there. Communications came from organized women in Brazil. At home, opportunities for contact with other national organizations rapidly enlarged.

The commission launched its work by a series of area, state, and large city meetings and soon established contact with the scattered state and local missionary unions. The affiliation of new groups came in rapidly that winter; the evidences of interest in a national movement exceeded expectation. Women had now fully assumed the initiative in it, with a group of able volunteer women giving it unstinted and devoted service.

---

* The New York *Times,* June 2, 1928.

The real significance of what church women were doing in the nineteen-twenties was more than organizational, however, important as the achievement of national identity and recognition obviously was to them.

In a decade when general interest in social reform was at its lowest ebb, and in the minds of most churchmen the Christian ethic had no relevance to the new social problems which the rapid changes of the post-war years were bringing, church women in their united local groups pioneered in attempting to meet these new needs.

Through the years when America had become strongly isolationist, the continuing interest of church women in missions helped to keep alive in the Church the Christian ideal of world-wide brotherhood and service. Their promotion of the World Day of Prayer, particularly, fostered this sense of fellowship with women around the world, whatever their race or nation.

National recognition had been won for an organization based not on a strictly denominational or interdenominational pattern but on the wider one of individual membership as Christians. Women's awareness of a common bond of faith underlying their work and binding them together carried ecumenical implications that were important. The wider fellowship which this conception made possible among members of local groups at home and with Christian women abroad was a new and stimulating experience. It opened up exciting possibilities and new ways by which church women could serve the immediate present and the future.

CHAPTER 3

Experiments in Co-operation
1929-1937

HARDLY had the National Commission of Protestant Women settled into its new offices in New York City, however, before it became evident that its path would not be as smooth or its prospects as bright as they appeared to be in June, 1928. Within a year it was being challenged by a division of opinion from within as to its autonomy, and from without by the onset of the worst economic depression that the country had ever known.

As it launched its new program, the commission seemed to be assuming the posture of a full-fledged national organization, complete with elected officers, a general secretary, a budget of its own, and a spread of committees. Yet in the minds of some of its most loyal supporters, there was a real question as to whether it was technically anything more than a glorified joint committee representative of old, well-established interests—home missions, foreign missions and local interdenominational groups. The commission had been empowered to act as a "Guiding Group," but certainly not to go off entirely on its own!

The two mission bodies, in particular, adopted a cautious and sceptical attitude toward the metamorphosis that seemed to be taking place before their very eyes. Even before the Buffalo meeting took place, the Federation of

Women's Boards of Foreign Missions had taken pains to amend its original action to approve the creation of a guiding group in these apprehensive words: "In voting to recommend to the constituent boards the co-operation now under consideration, we do so upon condition that this is an experiment for three years from June, 1928. If during that period the experiment be found not to work to the best advantage of those great interests that have been intrusted to us as a federation, we shall be free to withdraw without any resulting disturbance of the friendly relationships which do and should exist among those engaged in Christian work."*

The federation and the Council of Women for Home Missions now repeatedly warned that "the commission is not an organization. Its duties are advisory only." They made it plain that they did not approve of the name "Commission," but preferred some such title as "Joint Advisory Committee on Church Women's Programs." To give birth to an independent young organization with ideas for developing a social program might jeopardize the wholehearted support of the missionary enterprise that had been built up through so many years. It was better not to risk the possibility.

The commission itself, in all its literature, was careful to avoid the use of the controversial phrase, "national organization." It had no wish to break relationship with the mission bodies. After all, were not its chairman and vice-chairman leading members of those very bodies?

The larger and more vocal affiliated local groups took a different point of view. As we have seen, many of these had long since been carrying on programs and activities that were more diversified than missions and stressed the social service needs in local communities. During the Buffalo meetings of 1928, their representatives met in a business

* From the minutes of a meeting of the Federation of Women's Boards of Foreign Missions, dated January 9, 1928.

session of their own, organized themselves, and elected Mrs. James T. Ferguson, a woman of unusual gifts of leadership, from Kansas City, as their president, giving her power to appoint a secretary. They felt that this was necessary in order that local groups might have some corporate voice in the deliberations of the commission. After this organization took place, the influence of the local groups increased as a factor to be reckoned with. In the minds of some, the commission was identified with the policy of the mission bodies which was felt to be conservative and too dominating a check on what local groups wished to do. Others, in despair, felt that differences were becoming so deep that it might be impossible ever to gather church women into one united organization. It was a difficult year.

The internal tension generated by all of this came to a head on June 15, 1929, when the first annual meeting of the National Commission of Protestant Women convened at the Hotel Bellevue in Boston. As had happened the previous year, the representatives of local groups met in a business session of their own in the same hotel, the same day. The attendance at the latter meeting was much larger than had been anticipated and it was clear that a crisis of some kind was in the making. Pressure in the country for a genuinely autonomous movement was too strong to be either ignored or suppressed. Genuine concern for the values at stake, personal factors, and a good deal of both confusion and enthusiasm were involved in it. By a humorous bit of irony, which did not help make things any clearer, the chairman of the commission and the chairman of the local groups were both named Ferguson!

At their first business session, the local groups re-elected Mrs. James T. Ferguson president, voted to endorse the work of the National Commission for the past year, and meticulously pledged to it their continued support. At their second session they seized the initiative by adopting for their own group a new and ambitious name, "The National

Council of Federated Church Women," thus clearly indicating their determination to identify themselves as a national, autonomous organization. Acting in their new name they then proceeded to set up a Relationships Committee of their own. This latter committee lost no time in recommending a merger of the new body with the National Commission of Protestant Women, to become operative not later than one year hence, in June, 1930. The recommendation was immediately passed with the proviso that after that date the new name, "National Council of Federated Church Women," should apply to the whole body.

This bold and ingenious proposal for refashioning the commission into something "closer to the heart's desire" aroused an enthusiasm that was irresistible. It was intended that the proposal to work out a correlation between the new body, the Federation of Women's Boards of Foreign Missions and the Council of Women for Home Missions be approved by the two latter groups before making the action public. But silence was impossible. Word of the joyful prospect leaked out to the country and the country happily assumed that what was hoped for had been in fact accomplished. It was of particular delight to the local groups to feel that the whole movement among church women would now be put into a positive and independent context.

The two mission bodies could hardly help being embarrassed by all this. To their great credit, they rose generously to the occasion. They not only recognized the National Council of Federated Church Women as the accredited channel by which they would henceforth have contact with local interdenominational groups of church women, but in the end handsomely promised to help the new organization by some financial subsidy for the next two years.

In respect to another important interdenominational body, the Federal Council of Churches, the new NCFCW (as we shall call the National Council of Federated Church Women for the sake of brevity) became more completely independent organizationally than it really intended to be. An action taken at Boston requested affiliation with the Federal Council of Churches. No direct affiliation was ever granted, although until 1941, the president of the NCFCW was included in the membership of its Administrative Committee.

ONE gathers that the events in Boston did not occur without some internal friction. Strong emotions and differences were involved but reports have treated them kindly. One records merely that "the name of the organization was changed," and Mrs. John Ferguson's wholly charitable account assures us that "the programs of both the local groups and the national commission were carried through to completion in perfect harmony." These were Christian ladies all, brave enough to face differences but eager to forget them afterwards, wanting above all to be found on the side of the angels in regard to the churches and the cause of missions to which they were devoted, but sensing that the angels were leading them invisibly along a new and untried path. Now that the main point had been unexpectedly solved, they looked to the future rather than the past. They were stirred with a conviction that was to remain with them that somehow, in ways they did not yet know, they had been "brought to the kingdom for such a time as this." It was both a sobering and an exciting moment.

Various technical hurdles still needed to be overcome. If the process now sounds over-meticulous, it bears witness to the care that these women took to spare each other's feelings and to proceed carefully. In February, 1930, Mrs. James T. Ferguson formally resigned as head of the local groups and Mrs. John Ferguson was elected in her stead, thus becoming leader of both these and the commission. In March, the commission met for the last time and "voted authoritatively to dissolve." Mrs. John Ferguson's description of this solemn moment reflects a general relief that the last delicate corner had been turned with appropriate dignity. "It was," she recorded, "like the passing of the Old Year and the coming of the New. I had gone to the meeting as president of one body and returned as president of another." Once again a united organization was on its way.

But if inwardly everything was now serene, outwardly it was not. American society as a whole was in trouble. A less auspicious time than the spring of 1930 to launch an organizational experiment dependent upon voluntary contributions for support could scarcely have been found in the history of the country.

The stock market crash of October 15, 1929, had started a downward spiral in the American economy which grew steadily worse with each succeeding month. The Great Depression caught most Americans unawares, though it had been in the making during the unhealthy boom period that preceded it. The transition from prosperity to hard times came on the country with almost unbelievable rapidity. Production fell as sales decreased, factories were forced to close, and unemployment spread more and more widely. Mortgages were foreclosed, banks refused loans, and the smaller banks began to fail. Within a year there were few people who were not affected adversely by the depression.

And the end was not yet. By 1932, some churches as well as many more banks and businesses were failing to meet their obligations. Church offerings dropped almost 50 per cent between 1930 and 1934. Budgets of churches and those of religious organizations had to be drastically reduced. At the same time, churches and service organizations were called on for charity to an extent that strained their resources to the limit. Pastors and employed staff spent more and more time trying to locate jobs for people in need. Religious papers were published less frequently and missionaries began to come home. Even a well-established organization like the Federal Council of Churches found its funds drastically reduced. A new and untried group like the NCFCW without financial resources or experienced leadership would obviously be faced with major difficulties.

Historians of this era lay emphasis on the fact that the depression which paralyzed the country for more than three years was psychological as well as financial. "Depression," wrote one of them, "meant not only 'hard times,' in the simple financial sense, but a deep, continuing and pervasive spiritual gloom." Perhaps the secret of the survival of the NCFCW during these lean years lay not only in the fact that women were more accustomed than their husbands to "shoe-string financing" and complete dependence upon voluntary service of all kinds, but also in the fact that the strong sense of purpose and meaning which continued to motivate these church women kept them from "spiritual gloom." Whether they were more optimistic by nature or merely more sheltered does not matter. What is striking is the fact that we have no record of local groups going out of existence because of the depression. On the contrary, there are evidences that they exerted a stabilizing influence by developing new and practically helpful service projects in their communities. The Rochester, New York, group, for example, helped canvass the churches to secure jobs for the unemployed in 1931 and 1932, and co-operated in visiting 5,000 families in a Work Relief Project. At the same time local groups, through their World Day of Prayer offerings, kept up much needed financial support to missionary projects.

CERTAINLY the national officers had no intention of postponing the pursuit of their national plans until normalcy returned. In 1932, the national office was moved from New York to Kansas City, Missouri. Many felt that it was a wise idea to locate the office in the center of the country where, as the one link between widely scattered groups, it might be geographically more accessible to all.

Kansas City was a natural choice since it was the home city of Mrs. James Ferguson, who, in 1932, succeeded Mrs. John Ferguson as the national president of NCFCW. Here modest office space was secured and one secretary helped carry the work. It was no inconsiderable undertaking. In her report to the next annual conference in Chicago in May, 1933, Mrs. Ferguson described how it was managed: "The fact that we had no money to pay the rent presented a serious problem. We went to our good friend who owns the R. A. Long Building and asked him if he would permit us the use of an office free of charge for four months. . . . Being successful in that effort we asked him if he would furnish a room for us. This also he consented to do. Additional furniture was borrowed, and we have been able to make some purchases since. . . . We believe the National Council is worthy of the most attractive surroundings possible. . . . I was exceedingly anxious to make it possible for the National Council to liquidate its indebtedness. . . . To the latter end I put the office secretary on half time and succeeded in getting the office rent reduced for a period of four months. On these two items we realized a saving of $2,175, which paid for the expense of promoting Dedication Day and left $25 in the Treasury." With such qualities, a woman's organization could survive anything!

"Dedication Day" was an inspired idea to provide a rallying point in the year for interest in the objectives of the national organization and personal sacrifice on its behalf. The first one was held in May, 1933, and was the beginning of the tradition of a May observance that would bring church women together in their own communities. Under a variety of names and different specific objectives this observance has persisted as a national event, and in 1945 became the present "May Fellowship Day." Like the Day of Prayer for Missions, it was a symbol of unity, and the "shower of dollars" which it brought was a welcome though very modest source of national support.

Another early source of support was affiliation dues of $5.00 annually. Only a few of the 1,300 local groups now listed were officially affiliated, and one of the tremendous tasks of the national office was to try to contact each one, to encourage affiliation, and then to help them as far as possible enrich and extend their existing programs. In her report of 1933, Mrs. Ferguson tells us that a letter was sent to all of these in the fall of 1932. One hundred eighty-six groups were considered affiliated but "84 are delinquent in the payment of annual dues, leaving 102 with dues paid to date."

The nadir of the depression was reached in the late winter of 1932-33 when with the general closing of the nation's banks fear as well as distress gripped the country. The memorable inaugural address of President Franklin Roosevelt on March 4, 1933, brought the first dawn of hope. The story of the recovery that followed in the next months is well-known, but it was only gradually that the cloud lifted and confidence and relative well-being were restored to the country as a whole.

At the annual spring meeting of 1934, Mrs. James Ferguson felt enough encouragement to put in a plea for a mimeograph machine. Thirty women replied with contributions—and the machine arrived, heralding a new day. With understandable pride she reported in 1935 that 75,000 sheets of material had been run off and distributed!

By the fall of 1934, it was possible to look forward to the future with less financial apprehension. But even so it must have taken faith as well as imagination to launch out in that year on the experiment of producing a regular official publication for country-wide use. The *News Bulletin*, printed in Kansas City, first appeared in November, 1934. It was to be published quarterly "to present a cross-section of the work of National Headquarters and of affiliated groups." From the beginning the new venture was successful, though it entailed the salary of an editor, Miss Louise

Deacon, who had had experience on an Oklahoma City daily paper. By supplying a regular channel of communication with local women's groups, the *News Bulletin* and its successor, *The Church Woman,* helped forge the link that held them together during these difficult years.

Items in the first issue indicate that NCFCW had already attained recognition as an influential national organization, and that it was actively involved in the contemporary crisis:

> Mrs. James T. Ferguson recently went to Washington as the representative of the NCFCW at the joint meeting of the Citizens Committee headed by Newton D. Baker, and the Woman's Committee headed by Mrs. Franklin D. Roosevelt.
>
> Regardless of public relief for those able to work but unable to find it, private relief must still go on in every community. . . .

But could the budget be increased in a depression year? The finance committee submitted detailed recommendations for raising it to $10,000, in order to "lengthen and strengthen the lines during 1934-35."

This plea did not go unheeded, for in February, 1935, Mrs. Ferguson announced gratefully that a group of six women had undertaken to underwrite the work. Each of the six guaranteed expenses of one month, pledging herself to secure a specified sum. Finances were constantly precarious and, like those of many another early women's organization, depended ultimately upon the loyalty and continuing sacrificial effort of generous women who believed that what NCFCW stood for was too important to let its work be curtailed.

The *News Bulletin* of February, 1935, also sounded a note of spiritual warning against undue complacency in the midst of its gratitude for improving conditions. The combination of hope and realism, of humility and capacity for sustained effort is so typical of the character of those who have made up the membership of the movement through the years, that we quote from a statement of the Spiritual Life Department:

> With the improvement of economic conditions, let us not allow our people to lose track of things spiritual from their lives.
>
> Have you allowed any financial depression to injure first of all your greatest enterprise, the evangelization of the world, while you kept yourselves safe and snug at home?

The suggestion followed that local councils celebrate Dedication Day on Ascension Day because "it was then that the church received her mandate to evangelize and Christianize all areas of life." For the first time printed programs for Dedication Day were now to be prepared in advance "free to all groups affiliated with the council—3 cents per copy to other groups."

One of the survival qualities that women who organized for idealistic purposes seemed to possess was a realistic understanding that spiritual dedication was related to financial responsibility. Always, they believed, these two must go hand in hand. The next issue stated this as a principle: "A budget for Christian work should be dealt with as a spiritual, not a material problem, for such it is. The spiritual success of an organization such as ours, depends to a very large degree on the financial support of *every* member." The tone of optimism increased as a plan was worked out during 1935, by which the budget could be met by regular support from members, as well as special gifts from sponsors. By 1936, reports from every officer and department were so encouraging that it could be fairly assumed that the depression, at least in its financial aspects, was a thing of the past.

As the NCFCW together with the rest of the country moved out from under the shadow of hard times, the social concern which it had inherited from the local groups in 1929 came into its own. The general climate of opinion in the country, and not least in church circles, was more favorable to social action.

For Americans as a whole had learned much from the depression years. They had learned that prosperity was not guaranteed, and that there were weak spots in the American life that demanded attention. And now, with rumblings of war in Europe, it was evident that neither peace nor democracy was guaranteed either. Discussions of the social implications of the Christian faith, sober and more realistic than in 1917, became popular at church conferences and many denominations set up national committees on social action. Interests in which church women had earlier pioneered seemed now on the way to becoming official in the accepted programs of the churches.

Through the rest of the nineteen-thirties, NCFCW was experimenting with ways of working toward the distinctly social objective stated in the constitution: "The task of establishing a Christian social order in which all areas of life shall be brought into harmony with the teachings of Jesus Christ." What progress did the women make?

They exerted an influence on public opinion by initiating specific projects. Certain social problems from the beginning aroused their special interest; in these they did remarkably effective pioneer work which was later taken over by other agencies. Improvement of moving pictures was one of these. Church women across the country became thoroughly aroused as to this need, and were able to bring considerable pressure to bear in many local communities.

In Southern California, appropriately enough, women seem to have taken the lead in this. Not content with general concern over Hollywood productions, they worked on concrete methods and proposals for raising their standards. At the executive meeting of their council in August, 1934, it was voted to establish a Board of Review comprised of eighty women "each of whom was delegated to spend two hours each month in pre-viewing films at Hotel Roosevelt in

Hollywood." From reports made by these women, the chairman of the Department of Pictures and Drama undertook the responsibility of issuing "a monthly list of film productions that are to be approved or boycotted by 400,000 women members of Protestant churches on the east coast." According to a later report, thirteen denominations, along with Catholic and Jewish groups, co-operated in the Southern California effort, which by 1936 had adopted a slogan "Select Your Moving Picture Entertainment," and claimed that "our allies in this are 23 million church women."

Not only California was involved. The state council president in Indiana toured her state in 1935 in the interests of better moving pictures and in the East, many groups adopted a "Declaration of Purpose on Wholesome Motion Pictures." In one city, the goal was to secure the signatures of 100,000 people, "including young persons" who would pledge themselves to "be alert in the choice of moving pictures; stay away from those morally questionable; stay away from those that make an unwholesome advertizing appeal."

Other local groups worked for the establishment of Friday and Saturday night "Family Night programs" of clean pictures suitable for family showing. A report printed in the February, 1936, *News Bulletin* asserts with satisfaction:

> Several thousand theatre owners have inaugurated in their theatres the Friday Family Night Program. . . . There seems little doubt that the improvement in pictures, so noticeable in the past year, is in large part the result of the policy pursued by Protestant church women and later, the Legion of Decency (Catholic). It would seem that the pendulum has begun its backward swing.

Mrs. Jesse M. Bader of New York, a national vice-president during this period, was especially interested in the subject of moving pictures. She did much to co-ordinate this interest and to develop the work of an able national committee to review and evaluate films. Her work led directly in the next decade to the establishment of the Protestant Motion Picture Council.

Another special and continuing concern of these years was peace. The shadow of a new war was beginning to fall across Europe, and America had learned by experience that the desire for peace was not enough to insure any country against war. The cause of war must be understood and the steps to peace found and patiently pursued. NCFCW co-operated actively in publicizing the radio talks of Dr. Walter Van Kirk, secretary of the Department of International Justice and Goodwill of the Federal Council of Churches, and prepared a study course on "Prospects for Peace." When the first Conference on the Cause and Cure of War was set up in Dallas in February, 1935, the Texas council was one of its early and most active supporters. When Major General Smedley Butler's book, *War Is a Racket*, appeared, the women revealed their leanings not only by recommending it, but by offering to furnish copies through the national office "in lots of 1,000 copies at 25 cents each," because it "supplies new thunder against war to add to the spirited agitation the NCFCW has been carrying on."

There were many other projects in the field of international relations. When Michi Kawai, the well-known woman leader of Japan, toured the cities of the country in 1934 in the interest of better relations with Japan, NCFCW had an important part, in co-operation with the Women's Committee of the Foreign Missions Conference, in setting up the meetings. It did the same the next year for Dr. Ida Scudder of Vellore Christian Medical College, India. For a time it looked as if some organizational relationship might develop between American church women and Christian women in India. It did not seem wise, however, for the national organization to encourage an international federation.

The 1935 annual meeting in Rochester, New York, seems to have been a turning point in the fortunes of NCFCW.

With the return of better times there was a good attendance of delegates. Mrs. Harper Sibley, president of the local group, was prominent in the city and planned an ambitious program of meetings and social events "in lilac time." The theme of the meetings, "Frontiers of a Christian Social Order," emphasized the social program of the organization, and a combination of publicity and prestige gave it impetus. State councils were encouraged; Texas and Georgia had been organized in 1934, Nebraska and Iowa, in 1935, and others followed.

However, the building of a general unified program of work had suffered during this post-war period, for understandable reasons. There was no national staff to help with this. NCFCW had the bewildering number of twelve program departments. The chairmen and members of these were volunteers, interested and devoted but living in widely separated cities. The amazing thing is not that confusion resulted but that so much was accomplished. The national office had to depend heavily on co-operative arrangements with denominational organizations for the preparation and promotion of program material. The program on missions, for example, was carried on in co-operation with the two interdenominational women's mission bodies. The program on race was carried through the Race Relations Department of the Federal Council of Churches, and world relations through the latter's Department of International Justice and Goodwill, later with the Cause and Cure of War Conference and the National Peace Conference. Joint committees planned for the World Day of Prayer, mission conferences and schools of missions, international relations, and peace.

It will readily be seen why such a pattern of work would not long be satisfactory for women who above all wanted united work to be "effective." They felt caught in a network of relationships which, however good from the angle of co-operation nationally, were too diffuse to result in the kind of impact that they felt was needed locally. The right pattern did not immediately emerge, but after the Rochester meeting it was evident that some steps, at least, in the direction of a better plan of work needed to be taken.

The annual meeting in Dayton, Ohio, in May, 1936, added to the momentum. "Never surpassed in the history of the council," according to the account in the first issue of *The Church Woman* in this year, it was an event that attracted delegates from Washington to Maine and from Florida to California. "Exploring and Possessing the Unclaimed Areas of Life in Citizenship, Personal Living, World Peace and Economics" was its theme. A social creed dealing with these subjects was debated and adopted. Women felt that the opportunities opened up at this meeting were deeply significant for the future of their movement and of the Church. The *News Bulletin* expanded to a magazine of twelve pages in July, 1936, and took a new name, *The Church Woman*. The first issue was devoted to the Dayton meeting: "vibrant with power, . . . expressive of deep conviction and able thinking. . . ."

At least one man among those who were present as observers at Dayton felt this also. In an editorial entitled "Watch Those Women!", Dr. Harry C. Munro, secretary of the International Council of Religious Education, wrote: "Non-ecclesiastical agencies or movements have a spontaneity, a freedom, a vitality which enables them to make a distinctive contribution to the Christian movement. . . . Watch these women. Here are a power, a radiance, a dedication of talents and service, a social idealism, and passion which are sorely needed by our Christian movement."

Among the actions taken at Dayton was one authorizing the setting up of a Re-evaluation Committee, of which Mrs. Sibley became chairman. A professionally trained worker was employed to make a survey of NCFCW. After a careful study, department by department, she recommended a simplification of the whole structure: "Fewer departments, with less time spent in co-ordinating work, would allow more time for actual work." At the next national assembly, at Lake Geneva, in July, 1937, a revised constitution was adopted, with some immediate changes which looked in this direction.

NCFCW was one of the agencies which had helped to launch the United Christian Adult Movement of the International Council of Religious Education the previous year. Working closely with the Adult Movement it adopted the pattern of "Seven Areas of Work": The Bible in Life; Personal Faith and Experience; Christian Family Life; Christian Church Life and Outreach; Community Issues; Major Social Relations; World Relations. These areas seemed to cover most of the work already being carried under other headings, and had the advantage of being more in line with general church programs. They did represent some simplification, and this pattern of the "Seven Areas" was followed until 1941. But in the end, this attempt to fit united women's work into the pattern of the Christian Adult Movement proved to be one more experiment in co-operation rather than a permanently useful plan.

In 1937, after five years in Kansas City, national headquarters moved to Chicago, where the new offices at 6200 South Kimbark Avenue were more ample and convenient. Miss Daisy June Trout of Indianapolis succeeded Mrs. J. N. McEachern of Atlanta as president of the NCFCW in this year, and proved her remarkable versatility by acting also as the council's executive and as the temporary editor of *The Church Woman*. The latter had already become a monthly magazine, and grown to twenty-four pages; its place of publication also moved to Chicago, and with a subscription list of upwards of two thousand, it continued to be the important channel of communication between the national office and the country.

In 1938, for no reason, apparently, other than that it was

awkward and unnecessary, the word "Federated" was dropped from the title of the national organization and it now became officially the "National Council of Church Women."

Most of the 250 local groups which were now affiliated with the national movement had by this time adopted the designation of "council" to conform with the "National Council" name. Certain characteristics of united work among women in the churches had already become clear in the period since its founding. One was its insistent social emphasis. At times this seemed to be in conflict with the traditional interest in missions, but a constant effort had been made to reconcile this conflict, in the belief that both were important and that they could and should be included in a larger view of Christian responsibility. This emphasis was basic in the purpose: "To unite church women in the task of establishing a Christian social order in which all areas of life shall be brought into harmony with the life and teachings of Jesus Christ." This latter statement is interesting also because its final phrase was borrowed from ecumenical sources, and witnesses to the close link which women's united work had with the latter from an early date. In pursuing a general social objective women had proved themselves capable of organizing special projects effectively.

Another characteristic was the desire to be a part of any general forward movement of the Church. "Women in the United Christian Advance" was the theme of the eighth annual conference at Lake Geneva in 1937. For a number of years the National Council of Church Women continued to hold annual meetings at Lake Geneva, following meetings of the Federal Council and the United Christian Adult Movement, in order that women might take advantage of these. When the "Preaching Mission of the Churches" was inaugurated women were active participants.

Organizationally, church women were trying to find themselves during these years. They hardly knew as yet in what their identity consisted, and certainly not what their unique contribution, if any, would be. They were sure they had been right in uniting. But what was to be the pattern of their work? Was it to be merely one of co-operation with existing church organizations? Would a generally co-ordinated program best serve the needs of the thousands of women in local councils? Only experience could tell them. It was this experience that the nineteen-thirties supplied. Out of the experiments we have been describing and well before the close of the decade, clues to the answer began to be found.

CHAPTER 4

The Pattern Emerges
1937-1946

Even before the new constitution was adopted at the annual meeting at Lake Geneva in 1937, many of the leaders of NCFCW had come to feel that the kind of changes which it proposed, while useful as an interim step, would not suffice permanently. Co-operation with other interdenominational church bodies would always be necessary. But for administering a program the present method was slow and cumbersome, because it necessitated referring every action of the joint committees back to the parent organizations for approval. Some organically unified structure seemed to be called for, strong enough and independent enough to allow decisions to be made and carried out promptly and effectively. But could the National Council of Church Women, the Council of Women for Home Missions, the Women's Committee of the Foreign Missions Conference ever become one united organization? The internal difficulties in the way seemed insurmountable.

A special committee on co-operation was set up at Lake Geneva to explore this faint hope. Three of the most experienced women from each of the three bodies, under the chairmanship of Miss Daisy June Trout, the newly elected NCFCW president, began what was to be a long process but one that showed increasing promise. A second stage was reached when this committee on co-operation was enlarged and reconstituted as the National Committee of Church Women at the beginning of 1938. Mrs. Katherine Silverthorn, whose wisdom and experience had already contributed so much to the development of united work, became chairman and the "National Committee" rapidly grew in importance as the symbol of a united movement.

The May Luncheons, promoted in local communities in 1938, were closely tied in with the new emphasis on unity. The May Luncheon idea had originated with the Council of Women for Home Missions in 1933 as a demonstration of the faith of women in the midst of a depression. Now it became a country-wide event geared to interpreting the significance of the National Committee of Church Women. A program was suggested featuring the history of the three organizations and a talk on "Christian Unity in Service." A national radio broadcast climaxed the occasion. The National Committee urged councils to set up luncheons that would not only be interdenominational, but would include near-by rural churches: "We have dreamed of the time when American church women could speak with one voice. Our efforts have sometimes been weakened by division. Sometimes the spirt has been more united than the channel through which it could flow. A larger sense of oneness of those who name the name of Christ is needed . . . that there may be a more unified approach to the problems of the world. Let May 3, 1938, be a day of new life and power." Enthusiastic reports poured in, showing that the event had been widely observed in forty-four states and Canada. The May Luncheon became an annual event.

What did all of this really mean? Certainly the coming together of women for service was not a new idea. This dream had been pushing them on for many years, as we have seen. But there was urgency in it now, and a prophetic note which gave a new, dynamic quality. The old tensions between missions and social action, which had plagued relationships between the national organization and the mission boards for so long, seemed to be swallowed up in a realization of the importance of women's task as a whole within the universal Church.

One reason for this, not to be underestimated, was the profound influence of the new theology and the ecumenical movement on the thinking of lay men and lay women in America following the world conferences on Faith and Order in Edinburgh, Scotland, and on Life and Work, in Oxford, England, during the summer of 1937. The leaders of the National Council of Church Women were educated and intelligent women, many of them deeply interested in the theological trends of the time and familiar with the ideas of such leaders as Niebuhr, Van Dusen, and Oldham. Ten American women, six of them official delegates, were among the relatively small group of women present at these conferences. Beginning with the October issue in that year, *The Church Woman* devoted considerable space to their reports on these important meetings. Ominous events in Europe, the shadow of a new war in the making, underlined the relevance of such statements as these: "Joining hands with churches around the world, and saying 'Our first allegiance is to God' will strengthen the Christians of the world in their determination to place God on the throne and relegate man and the nation to second place. . . . The chief trouble with today's world is that man has de-throned God and elevated self in God's stead, while disillusionment has led people to surrender authority over all life into the hands of the nation-state, with its symbolic head, the dictator." In line with such thinking, the theme chosen for the June, 1938, annual meeting at Granville, Ohio, was "The Christian Challenge to the Modern World."

To women it seemed an obvious step in this direction, and one which lay within their power, to join hands more firmly within the churches. "Let women in their church and interchurch relations disseminate a consciousness of the unity of Christ's cause. Too many sour prophets are making a wailing wall of the Church and spreading the pessimism that we are all shot to pieces and divided. . . . Let us breathe the atmosphere of sacred unity in one Lord. . . . Women can also infuse the ecumenical spirit into practical programs of missions, education, peace, organizations, social service, and federations of churches." From the intellectual and theological side, ideas such as these were germinal to the new plan. Women knew they were a part of the Church Universal, and wanted to witness to its reality at a dark moment in the world's history by being "one" among themselves.

Closely related to this was the idea that women had a larger potential contribution to make to the total life of the Church than had ever been realized. Effective organization could help rouse women on the one hand and churches on the other to this fact. The chairman of *The Church Woman* committee expressed it this way in a September, 1939, editorial:

> Women are ready to stand by the church, to minimize its obvious weaknesses and to emphasize its latent powers; to give to it, to work for it, to pray that it may be a tool of God. Church women form a group of more than 15,000,000 in the U.S.A., yet they are without a voice. The voice of the official church is still largely a man's voice, for what church is governed equally by its men and women members?

This seemed to be true even in so liberal an organization as the Federal Council of Churches, where women sat on boards and committees. Men felt that there was no reason for women to feel at a disadvantage, but women felt that they had little real participation in policy-making. Rightly or not they felt that when they offered suggestions "men waited politely, then proceeded just as if they had not spoken." The Woman's Co-operating Commission of the Federal Council of Churches, appointed in 1936, was solely for the purpose of building up support among women for its budget and defending its program. But the program as a whole did not seem to include their thinking, though women heartily endorsed its value.

As yet no factual studies of women's place within the Church, such as appeared a decade later, had been made, but by 1938 women had considerable organizational experience behind them, as well as opinion to share about matters that touched the whole life of the Church. If they could "speak with one voice" on such concerns, they might be the better heard. And so indeed it proved.

But aside from theological and emotional reasons, there were important practical reasons for the consolidation of women's interests. The future development of united work locally was at stake. Local groups had been historically the reason for a national organization, and the National Council of Church Women saw clearly that they not only continued to be its life-blood, but that any effective united work depended directly upon them. Women needed to act together at the local level quite as much as at the national level, and to organize on the committee pattern. So far, the national organization had been able to help very little directly in this. An "Inter-Council Field Department" had indeed existed among the co-operating interdenominational organizations, but the relationships and procedures were exceedingly complicated, and little real field service to women's groups resulted. More guidance was needed for their development than a loose federation could supply. The Federal Council of Churches was not contemplating plans for promoting the organization of women's groups, and moreover did not operate to any extent in the South. Many women's groups did not wish to federate with them locally. But if cultivated, many more than the 250 affiliated groups would join a national women's organization. At least 1,500 potential groups were known to exist. The "fields were white" for a great forward movement of women within the churches, but leaders rightly saw that better planning and much more attention to administrative detail must facilitate the harvest that lay ready.

The National Committee continued its explorations. A year later at Red Bank, New Jersey, May, 1939, it was ready to call together the official boards of the three women's organizations to take action. The Red Bank meeting approved the creation of a single national body which would take over all the functions relating to local interdenominational groups and "find a way in which church women can think and act together as a unit of the Church Universal."

Some criticism was to be expected of such a move, and the Red Bank meeting asked itself a crucial question. Would such action, in effect, separate women into a special "bloc" within the Church? The women expressed their point of view in a crucial answer. No, they said, a better integrated organization will serve to arouse the women as well as correlate their efforts. Far from separating them, it can show them how better to play their part in the whole Church!

Following this decision to go ahead, a Planning Committee of the National Committee was commissioned to draw up a detailed plan. The country waited while it considered alternatives. A tentative plan of union was submitted in January, 1940, discussed, revised, and submitted to the parent boards. These met at Swarthmore in June, 1940, for final revisions, which then had to be approved by the separate annual meetings of the three organizations. The country was kept in touch by progress reports in *The Church Woman*. "Do not grow impatient with what may seem a long and tedious process," Mrs. Silverthorn cautioned in March. "So momentous a step needs much careful planning and consultation. But be encouraged. We are making good progress. Keep a steady mind . . . God will lead us as we seek his guidance in what seems the inevitable step toward closer unity, a consummation long desired by many of us."

The careful process was at last completed. The final annual meeting of the National Council of Church Women was held in June, 1941. Miss Mary Smith, an Episcopal leader from Minneapolis who had served as president since 1939, and had worked tirelessly to bring all the groups together, was empowered to continue in office until the new organization was established. Many different names were considered for the latter, but the one chosen was "The United Council of Church Women." The change from "national" to "united" correctly summed up the complex of reasons for its coming into existence. So did the new wording of the purpose. Through subsequent revisions and changes, this purpose has since remained constant: "To unite church women in their allegiance to their Lord and Savior, Jesus Christ, through a program looking to their integration in the total life and work of the church, and to the building of a world Christian community."

One hundred delegates were appointed from the three organizations to come together at a Constituting Convention in Atlantic City, December 11-13, 1941. "The future is thrilling to contemplate!" said a statement prepared for those asked to accept this responsibility. "Now at last real union is possible. What a group of women—almost the total force of womanhood in the Protestant churches—can do if they set their minds to it! This really *can* transform the world. . . . But they must be prepared to share the grimmer reality this world has come to mean."

Grim reality, as well as elation and dedication, did indeed have a place in this historic meeting.

Strangely enough, as had happened in 1929, a high moment again coincided with a profound crisis in the life of the nation as a whole. The attack on Pearl Harbor occurred on December 7 while women were packing to set out for Atlantic City, and while they were still in the convention war was declared. Without any of the elation that had marked the entry into World War I, America accepted the fact that the winning of World War II must now be her first concern, demanding all her energies and resources.

It was strange, too, that the first official communication of the new United Council of Church Women, which had worked so long and consistently to build for peace, should have had to do with its participation in a war. But as in the rest of the nation, there was no hesitation in the response to this crisis. A telegram was sent to the President at once: "The newly constituted United Council of Church Women, representing ten million women of seventy Protestant communions, pledges its loyalty to the highest ideals of our nation in this hour of grave crisis."

It might seem an inauspicious moment for moving forward to fulfill the plans so long in preparation. But there was the general feeling that a united Christian front was needed now more than ever. The war must of course be taken into account, but real progress need not be halted. There was permanent significance and value in what had come to pass at Atlantic City, and this would remain.

A letter dated December 18, 1941, to a generous donor who had sent $5,000 as a founding gift, reflects vividly the atmosphere of this meeting. "We had been at war only five days. Hearts were tense and minds anxious, yet even out of such circumstances one hundred women came as planned months before from all over the United States, with almost no absentees. The world was breaking around us, but here was a uniting force bespeaking a power that could keep bridges of friendship across all chasms now, and be prepared to take an active part in remolding later this molten world of ours."*

Women in the churches were now united as never be-

---

* Letter from Mrs. Emory Ross to Dr. and Mrs. Wm. Bancroft Hill. National files.

fore, whatever the tragedy of the times. It was in this spirit that a "call" was sent out from the Constituting Convention before it adjourned: "Meeting at this hour of our country's involvement in war and at the time of the world's greatest tragedy, we still believe individually and collectively that God reigns and that ultimately his will shall prevail. In deep penitence for our share in the world's guilt and woe, we call upon the women of the Church to enter with us into the sufferings and sacrifices of the human family

To combat the rising tide of hatred caused by war.

To minister to those suffering from the ravages of war.

To maintain and strengthen the Christian fellowship.

To show friendship and understanding to the men and women in service for the defense of our country.

To maintain the integrity of the home.

To continue to its fullest degree the ongoing ministry of the Church, even to the uttermost parts of the earth.

To consecrate ourselves to the task of demanding of our country that it assume its full responsibility in the days to come in helping build a world order based on love and justice without which there can be no durable peace."

Miss Amy O. Welcher of the Congregational Christian Churches, elected first vice-president, became acting president of the new organization until she was prevailed upon to accept the office of president at the first Assembly in December, 1942. The other elected officers were each from a different denomination.

Office space for the United Council of Church Women was secured at 156 Fifth Avenue, New York City, and in September, 1942, Mrs. Ruth Mougey Worrell, a Methodist from Columbus, Ohio, became executive secretary of the new organization, with the help of a clerk and a stenographer. With a wide knowledge of church interests, an instinct for the important, and the capacity to inspire those with whom she worked, Mrs. Worrell was ideally suited for this. The remarkable development which took place in the United Council of Church Women in the next five years was due in no small degree to her leadership.

UCCW, as we shall now refer to it, did not rush into changes in the program already under way. It inherited the work of active committees on International Relations, Race, Public Relations, and *The Church Woman* which now had 2,235 subscribers. The World Day of Prayer, observed in 7,000 communities in this country, was in the words of Margaret Applegarth, its able chairman for many years, "the most precious treasure to be turned over to this new organization." Observances in the fifty countries abroad continued to be the responsibility of the Woman's Committee of the Foreign Missions Conference. Yet the new freedom in decision and self-determining action brought changes, and the rate of change accelerated as the country responded to a new pattern of work. Mrs. Emory Ross became a member of the staff in 1942, as general assistant, and gradually others were added to both the professional and clerical staff. Mrs. Mabelle Rae Le Grand became editor of *The Church Woman* in 1943, and gave distinguished service in that capacity for nine years. Though the national staff never became large, it could supplement more adequately the services of the volunteer officers and committee members upon whom UCCW continued to depend.

UCCW was fortunate in its strong volunteer leadership during these creative years. Miss Daisy June Trout, for example, had been a national secretary for her denomination, the Disciples, with experience in the YWCA and a degree in social work. She was typical of many others no less well equipped through education and varied experience to give leadership. Miss Florence Tyler and Miss Sue Weddell from the Foreign Missions Conference, Miss Edith Lowry, Miss Emma Jessie Ogg, and Mrs. Norman Vincent Peale from the Home Missions Council, Mrs. J. D. Bragg, national president of the Methodist Society for Christian Service, Mrs. Abbie Clement Jackson of the A.M.E. Zion

Church and Mrs. Charles S. Johnson, Congregational Christian, Mrs. Herbert Crowe, Society of Friends, were but a few of many devoted leaders. Relations with the YWCA were close, and many of its able secretaries were among the volunteers.

THE first biennial Assembly of UCCW occurred at Cleveland, Ohio, December, 1942, only a few months after Mrs. Worrell's arrival as director. It was not large in numbers due to difficult wartime transportation, but it fulfilled its promise "courageously to survey the church woman's place in the war crisis and point up her alertness to the kind of peace that must follow." Its program illustrates the subjects that especially concerned UCCW during the war period: problems arising in camp and defense communities, the wartime problems of families, the spiritual implications of racial problems, sacrificial living and giving.

A War Emergency Committee was set up to clear national requests, and a Committee on Volunteer Workers for Defense Areas undertook to keep church women in touch with special local needs. Child care centers and daily vacation Bible schools were started by church women in many communities. On the west coast they worked in the relocation centers for wartime evacuees, and later, with a special sense of responsibility for our Japanese-Americans, gave active help in their resettlement. Church women worked as special counselors in camp and defense communities. In 1943, UCCW set up a special committee on Religious Ministrations to Women in the Services with Mrs. Samuel McCrea Cavert as chairman. There was a feeling that little was being done in this regard and that women serving as Wacs and Waves were making a contribution not only to the war efforts, but to women's place in our national life. Teen-age canteens were started in many communities to provide wholesome recreation for this age group. Women's response to a special appeal to local councils to give understanding help in this situation was said to have eased the tension in communities where churches frowned on dancing!

The amount of space devoted to international relations in *The Church Woman* during the war period bears witness to the deep concern felt by church women. In January, 1939, the National Committee had worked out a statement of principles called the "Church Woman's Decalogue of Peace" which it recommended to all local women as a basis for their efforts in this field. "War," it had declared, "should never be blessed or condoned as a means of settling international disputes." A revised statement in June, 1939, was more moderate: "We believe in international co-operation as the best means to prevent war and remove the causes of war. We believe the United States should consult with other nations in the event of war or the threat of war. We believe in reduction of armaments and control of the munitions industry by international agreement." Now, in 1943, a ten-point "Program for Church Women in a World at War" was worked out. An imaginative suggestion was made that Armistice Day in 1943 be set apart as a special "Peace Day," with a program on the theme: "The Price of Enduring Peace." A ballot to register opinion on certain questions was prepared, and 85,000 leaflets promoting the observance were distributed. Women gave an offering for the Church Committee on Relief and Reconstruction, and according to reports, cast more than 100,000 ballots.

With such great interest evident, it was proposed the following year that this observance become one of the "special days" annually in the church woman's program, to be known as "World Community Day" and observed on the first Friday in November each year. Mrs. Worrell secured the support of denominational women in this project and it was hoped that, like the World Day of Prayer, World Community Day might ultimately be observed internationally, binding church women together in a common search for peace that would endure. Its emphasis was constructive and aligned church women with the support of the United Nations whose charter would be signed in San Francisco in 1945. The second observance in 1944 was climaxed by the signing of the following personal pledge on the part of those who participated: "I do solemnly promise, in the presence of God, to work and pray for the establishment of a just and durable peace. I do this both for the sake of the future peace and prosperity of the United States of America, and for justice and liberty for the people of all nations. Unto this task I commit my will and my prayers."

In June, 1944, just before the war's close, UCCW was one of seventy-five organizations participating in a conference at the White House on "How Women May Share in Post-War Policy Making," sponsored by Mrs. Franklin D. Roosevelt.

In the years that followed, church women, as part of the World Community Day observance, collected tons of used clothing in co-operation with United Nations Reconstruction and Rehabilitation (UNRRA) and Church World Service drives. In 1947, Mrs. Harper Sibley, who had been elected president in 1944 to succeed Miss Welcher, went to Europe to see at first hand and report on the distribution and use of the vast quantity of material aid furnished by American church women.

Even through the war years, UCCW had the development of ongoing united work locally very much in mind. Its basic philosophy of membership was expressed in the constitution which defined the constituency of the national movement as "every Protestant woman in the United States." A statement of the Board in October, 1943, stated its objective in these words: "The primary function of UCCW is the organization and development of local and state councils in line with the objectives of the purpose. . . . The first step in building local program is to induce women to look at the needs of their communities and gird themselves to help meet those needs."

Denominational work was a factor on the local as well as the national scene and UCCW did not overlook this, though the relationship was never worked out in this period as carefully as it was to be later. The general philosophy in this regard was expressed in a statement in 1944: "UCCW does not seek to duplicate what denominations are doing, but only to provide a way for women of all denominations to unite their strength on issues too big for any one group. The aim is to draw women together in every community."

The old assumption that membership in the local councils of course included women from the Negro churches was never seriously questioned. There had been considerable discussion as to whether or not such a stipulation should be included in the new constitution. But it was decided that the Christian assumption underlying the long tradition that "interdenominational" unquestionably meant "interracial" was stronger if it did not seem necessary to put it into the constitution. But the assumption had been buttressed in the document by a specific qualification in regard to annual and regular meetings: "It is understood that such meetings shall be held under conditions in which there shall be no discrimination."

Good administration and good committee work began to be emphasized locally as well as nationally. Councils were encouraged to plan the year's work in advance, to analyze the qualities needed for effective chairmen of departments, and to work locally from a budget. The pages of *The Church Woman* at this period bristle with how-to-do-it suggestions intended for local council women. The exchange of ideas on the "There's a Way" page was especially popular. Not for some years would it be possible for the national office to produce a formal handbook because of the lack of standard program and practice, but state and national meetings were utilized to strengthen local work, and local presidents met together on special occasions to exchange ideas.

The cumulative effects of this cultivation and strengthening of council work at the "grass roots" soon became apparent and was one of the reasons for the phenomenally rapid growth of the united movement after the organization of UCCW. The growth was reflected spectacularly in the national budget. When Mrs. Worrell came to New York as the new executive secretary, the year's budget was $12,000. In 1943, it was $13,500, in 1944, $40,000, with a fund of $150,000 for a three-year program of expansion already under way, and in 1946, it reached $60,000. Only a part of this was from local councils, but the percentage was rising. Increased contributions from individuals and from May Fellowship Day helped. The latter had taken the place of the May Luncheons, and a third of the local offering was devoted to national support. In addition, the World Day of Prayer offering leaped from $84,000 in 1942 to $145,000 in 1944 and $184,000 in 1946, all of which was totally transmitted to the mission boards for the support of migrant work and Indian American schools at home, and for Christian colleges for women and Christian literature overseas. It was all very encouraging.

THE year 1945 was an important one in the midst of this rapid development. It was high time that UCCW paused a moment to take stock of both what had happened in the three and a half years since its founding, and whither it was now bound. A report in May of that year reviewed the high points. The number of local councils was now nearly seven hundred. Attendance at the second Assembly at Columbus in 1944 had reached six hundred. National board membership had grown from 81 to 134, and the number of national committees from six to fourteen. "With countless opportunities before it, UCCW could be overwhelmed or scatter its efforts. Or it could become a superficial goodwill organization, lacking skills and expertness in any chosen field." If it was really to help mold public opinion, it must give fresh thought to its distinctive function, its administration and its relationships. "For this, UCCW was born, and for this it must become a more perfect instrument."

On October 22, 1945, one hundred and fifty leaders, among them many state presidents, met in Washington for an expanded meeting of the board. It was the first time of meeting since the world was at peace, and it had been preceded by careful planning. In groups of ten, the women met with senators, representatives, and scientists to discuss current issues and the atom bomb. They were received for tea by President and Mrs. Truman, and for dinner at the American University at the home of President Douglass. The week, "the most important since the birth of UCCW," resulted in many decisions that were at once turned into action.

Some of the most important had to do with the recent acceptance of a substantial gift from the Rosenwald Fund, which necessitated the incorporation of the organization and a revision of its by-laws. The grant had been secured on the basis of the contribution of UCCW to the betterment of race relations. It would make possible for three years the employment of a full-time secretary in the field of industrial and race relations, and an expanded program. A new department, called Christian Social Relations, came into being with Mrs. Theodore O. Wedel, an Episcopalian from Washington, D. C., as volunteer chairman and Miss Louise Young as director. Miss Young was able to obtain leave from her position as teacher of sociology at Scarritt College. They proved an excellent team in working on such concerns as race, citizenship rights, education, the family, health and child welfare, and in helping councils make a beginning in building up local and state committees on Christian Social Relations.

These were exciting and creative years. In June, 1945, delegates of the nations met in San Francisco and signed the Charter which created the United Nations. Church women, through UCCW, worked hard to interpret this event and helped to build up a body of support for the United Nations within the churches. In the fall of 1945, they co-operated actively in arranging a series of radio broadcasts in local communities. Two of these were on the World Charter, two on World Community, and two on the World Church. Councils in ninety-six cities and thirty-eight states joined in sponsoring these broadcasts, which were climaxed by a nation-wide hook-up the last Sunday in October.

Miss Mabel Head resigned her position as vice-president of UCCW in order to accept the position of "official observer" at the United Nations. This made for a close continuing relationship and through the next years her able and detailed reports of the various facets of United Nations activities and deliberations were featured by *The Church Woman* each month and helped to keep women all over the country informed.

There was a general feeling that church women in the United States had a special responsibility to take the initiative in building up again an understanding relationship with the women of Japan. The "bomb that dropped on Hiroshima" must not continue to shatter that relationship. During these years there was much discussion of sending a delegation to Japan as a gesture of friendship and Christian concern. Mrs. Sibley and Mrs. Welthy Honsinger Fisher, who chaired the World Day of Prayer Committee, were only two of several who eventually went and reported back on the thinking of women in the "new Japan." There were church women too among the wives in the occupation forces, and one of the interesting results of all these contacts in Japan was the organization of an active group of American and Japanese Protestant women in Tokyo in 1947, which later became the "Tokyo Council of Church

Women." Leaders in this group pioneered in establishing "brides schools" for the Japanese wives of service men, and in work among Japanese children.

Another concern which developed during 1945 had to do with the great influx of students from foreign countries, beginning to come to the United States for training in special fields. The next year, 10,000 had come to American colleges and universities, and church women had the imagination to see that by opening their homes to these students and influencing community attitudes, they could make an important contribution to mutual understanding and to better relations with the countries from which they came.

These and other matters were taken up at the third National Assembly which met in Grand Rapids, Michigan, in November, 1946, with the largest attendance in the history of the national organization. A report of this entitled "No Speed Limit for 1947" indicates the mood in which it met. The feeling was general that Europe was weary and that America must take the lead in solving three great problems of security, food, and satisfactory relations between stronger and weaker peoples. A start on all this was now possible through the United Nations and church women were ready to respond to the opportunity open to them.

On the wings of new hope for a new day, the pattern for the national organization had now assumed a form that gave dynamic promise for the future. It would not, of course, ever be a static one so long as church women were responsive to the needs of the times. But the main outlines of a national-local structure and of a democratic way of working on needs and interests especially close to the hearts of church women seemed to have emerged.

The new national organization was both united and autonomous, though it worked in close co-operation with more than forty other national organizations. A truly responsible administration had been set up to which local groups could look for help, and which in turn would be responsive to their desires and interests. The beginning of leadership training appropriate to the development of this kind of democratic structure was already under way. Three major program departments had been created, under which program interests were naturally grouped: World Missions (soon to be renamed Christian World Missions), Christian Social Relations, and Christian World Relations. Each had its "special day," the observance of which served as the three focal points of the year, together with the study program which each encouraged. The long-cherished World Day of Prayer in support of missions occurred on the first Friday in Lent. May Fellowship Day attached to the Department of Christian Social Relations claimed the first Friday in May. World Community Day was already well-established on the first Friday in November as the culmination of a fall emphasis on Christian World Relations. Together they dramatized in recurring fashion women's wider interests in the Church, and supplied abundant opportunity for greater knowledge in regard to them and service and personal sacrifice in their behalf.

It was a structure sufficiently integrated to be coherent and effective yet flexible enough to allow for diversity of interests, for using the special capabilities of individuals, and for initiative on the part of the local groups that composed it. Church women had, organizationally speaking, found themselves.

CHAPTER 5

Challenge and Response

1946-1951

BUT winds from a different direction were already blowing. Well-launched as a free and independent movement and sailing speedily along on a course that seemed highly rewarding, the United Council of Church Women would gladly have disregarded them. But this was impossible.

Even before World War II, the suggestion had come from the International Council of Religious Education that a merger of all national interchurch organizations into a single corporate body should be considered. The ecumenical movement had influenced church thinking and planning in this country. Union of the Protestant churches in "faith and order" might never be possible or even desirable, in America. But surely much in the area of "life and work" could be carried on together to mutual advantage and would result in an increased impact on the secular world. If American Protestantism could speak with one voice at least on social questions, it would be a great step forward. Not all denominations could be expected to agree to this, but there was hope that opinion in the liberal churches would support it.

A committee met to consider the matter in May, 1940. UCCW was one of the interdenominational bodies invited to join its early deliberations, and was represented by

Miss Amy Welcher and Mrs. Fred Bennett. The others were all agencies with which UCCW had long had a co-operative relationship: the Federal Council of Churches, the Foreign Missions Conference of North America, the Home Missions Council, the International Council of Religious Education, the Missionary Education Movement of the USA and Canada, the United Stewardship Council.

A "Committee on Closer Relationships Among Inter-Church Agencies" seems to have functioned almost continuously from this time on, even during the war. The first draft of a possible constitution for a "North American Council of Churches" appeared as early as 1942. It was to be in no sense a "super-church" armed with authority, but a council created by action of the denominations which would constitute its membership. The eight interdenominational agencies would be the nucleus of the divisions and departments of its work. Already a World Council of Churches was on the verge of formation; it would be useful to have an American council to relate to the international body.

Could there be any question as to the attitude of UCCW toward such a union? United women's work had for decades operated on the principle that it was good to work across denominational lines. Members of UCCW were without question ecumenically-minded. They were sensitively aware of the trend of the times. Yet there *were* questions—searching questions. Many of those who cared most deeply about the future of organized united work were the most troubled.

The idea of a merger of men's and women's organizational church interests in an overarching structure was in effect a challenge to many presuppositions. The national organization had met various other kinds of crises—disapproval, financial trouble, controversy. But this merger challenged a value that seemed fundamental—women's independent action as a group. Was it possible to safeguard this freedom, which historically had opened up so many opportunities, and still merge in a combined organizational structure? UCCW did not want to be caught in the position of waving the banner of "women for women" within the Church. Yet was it possible to face all the questions that would be necessary, without raising the basic issue of women's place in all policy-making church bodies? Uniting with a National Council was not a decision for the hour or the year but for the whole future of women's united work. It could not be made without considering all of its implications.

Yet UCCW agreed with the purpose behind the merger, and was sensitive to its timeliness. The beaches of history, women knew full well, were "strewn with the dead bodies of organizations that had been caught swimming in the wrong direction." Now by a strange irony their own national organization, built up with such effort and sacrifice, seemed to be caught by conflicting loyalties poised above just such a beach! By 1947, it was obviously only a matter of time before the decision would have to be made. The recommendations of the Committee on Closer Relations had become detailed and some form of merger, with or without UCCW, appeared a certainty.

This was no time to let emotion rule. Only intelligent and objective thinking would discover a creative approach to the problem. Before we trace the steps which UCCW took, we need to look more closely at the situation as it appeared to the women.

There were, for example, the structural differences in the eight interchurch bodies. All except UCCW were organized on strictly denominational lines. UCCW had never thought of itself as an "agency" of the denominations, but as a "movement" among the women of the churches. Its program was appropriate to the latter conception, but hardly geared to run through denominational channels. Moreover, among the members of eighty-two denominations in its local membership were many Unitarians, especially in New England, and some others who could hardly be classified as "Protestant evangelical." Though in no sense an interfaith movement, UCCW felt that it was important to include in its membership any woman who wished actively to support its Christian purpose. What would be the attitude toward this inclusive policy?

There were other differences. With the exception of the Federal Council of Churches, the other agencies were purely national in scope and function. Even the Federal Council, which in 1942 had two hundred city and state units, was mainly oriented to a national program. The opposite was true of UCCW. Its real strength came from roots in local communities, and the secret of its recent growth had been the cultivation of local program. The number of councils had increased from 420 in 1941 to 800 in 1946 and 1,432 in 1948. Would this "grass roots" focus be understood? If hindered, could the movement remain vigorous?

As such questions were being weighed an event occurred of great importance to the whole Christian world, underlining on a world scale the trend toward greater Protestant unity. For UCCW it served, curiously enough, to bring out into the open where it could be objectively discussed, the very problem which was the main obstacle to becoming a constituent part of the proposed National Council.

The long-anticipated birth of the World Council of Churches took place at Amsterdam, Holland, in August, 1948. From forty-four countries, 147 communions joined in this latest evidence of the strength of the ecumenical movement. The significance of this made a tremendous impression, not least upon American church women who had been preparing for it in their own way.

A council woman from Rochester, N. Y., Mrs. Edwin Allen Stebbins, was a member of the Commission on Faith and Order of the World Council and of its American Committee. In the decade after Edinburgh and Oxford she and others had fostered ecumenical study groups as part of local council programs. By 1947, nearly a third of all the local councils had ecumenical committees which stimulated a knowledge of the basic beliefs of the churches in their midst and a sympathetic understanding of their ways of worship.* Council women, by the time of Amsterdam, were by no means ecumenically illiterate. Several UCCW women, including the president, were present at this historic meeting, and their reports, published in *The Church Woman*, were read with profound interest.

In response to requests from many countries, one of the first acts of the World Council was to authorize a commission on the "Life and Work of Women in the Church." A world-wide study of the subject was begun. Reports from more than fifty countries came in, indicating how widespread was the interest in the subject, and these were later compiled and evaluated by Dr. Kathleen Bliss of England in a book, *The Service and Status of Women in the Churches*. The study proved to be just the beginning, rather than the end, of an exploration which has continued fruitfully in the World Council ever since.

The American phase of the study was carried by a group of which Miss Rhoda McCulloch of the staff of the YWCA, representing the Federal Council, was chairman. Miss Inez Cavert of the Department of Research of the Federal Council compiled the report entitled *Women in American Church Life*, published in 1948, and widely read. The factual picture it presented of the present degree of women's participation in the policy-making bodies of national church agencies was not reassuring. There were in 1948, 538 men and 63 women on the board of the Federal Council chosen by the denominations, 313 men and 41 women on the International Council of Religious Education, 82 men

---

* Inez Cavert: *Women in American Church Life*, Federal Council of Churches, 1948.

and 10 women on the Stewardship Council. Numbers on the mission boards were more equally divided.

The place of women on governing boards of churches locally and regionally was roughly similar. Though women were rarely officially disqualified from serving, it was still almost as true as decades before that few actually did. Executive committees in many local federations of churches included few women, even when a council of women was the "woman's department" of the federation. One midwestern city reported that the only federation office held by a woman was that of second vice-president, with one woman among thirty-three men on the executive committee. The picture in the country varied widely, of course, but it raised an open question. If the participation of women was not real in fact but only in theory, was it a service either to women or to the Church for UCCW to give up its separate existence? What women could accomplish in their own organization had been proved. What their future would be in a general church body was not nearly so certain.

That women were feeling proud of their program in these years was obvious, and did not make the decision any easier. There was some basis for this organizational pride, as a quick look at the development taking place in the period 1946-1949 will show. Not all their attention or energy was by any means taken up by the question of the merger. Too much else that was urgent and important was happening. UCCW leaders, nationally and locally, were caught up in needs and situations that demanded more from them than ever before.

The first National Assembly after World War II, held in Grand Rapids in 1946, had generated new energy. The number of recommendations and plans it produced reflected the general feeling that a new era had opened full of new responsibilities and opportunities for America. Church people must not lag behind the national effort, but do their share of pioneering. Tomorrow was here. War's aftermath of human suffering must be met by America's help and leadership and new domestic problems faced.

Mrs. Sibley was re-elected president in 1946, as she would be once more in 1948. An expanded program of worship, study, and action was adopted and an increased budget accepted to undergird it. The latter was projected on a new basis—the acceptance by the state councils of a fair state-and-local share in financing the national movement. Giving up the old pattern of "annual dues" took courage but the new one recognized a more truly corporate sharing of common responsibility. The democratic basis of the movement was more than ever a reality. The stirring speech of Lillian Smith, "The Only Safe Thing Is to Take Risks," symbolized the mood of the meeting and the experience of a corporate communion service, with the voice of Rosa Page Welch, which was to become known among church women around the world, singing "Let Us Break Bread Together on Our Knees," symbolized its spirit of commitment.

UCCW members found that their outlook upon the world, as well as their capacities for leadership, was stretched as they tried to implement this program of "living one's faith." The remark of one member after a board meeting in October, 1947, "I have grown up this week," found an echo in the experience of many another woman involved in this burgeoning program.

THE emphasis of the period was on action. "Action follows study" became almost a slogan. The advice of one national chairman to her local groups was typical: "Never get so interested in your *subject*, what there is to say, that you forget your *object*, what there is to accomplish!"

World Community Day was a natural focus of study and activity in applying this principle to international relations. Know your United Nations by all means, and don't forget to study the Marshall Plan and Reciprocal Trade treaties.

But then, in your own community, help women to see that there are small practical ways within reach of their hands, by which they can help to build peace in the world.

In 1945, local councils coupled their study of "The Price of Enduring Peace" with the making of one million diapers and thousands of layettes for shipment overseas. In 1946, they sent half a million useful "Kiddie Kits" and 500,000 bundles of clothing to Europe through Church World Service. The study theme for 1947, "The World Is My Community," was coupled with the collecting of hundreds of thousands of "Pack-a-Towel" bundles of necessities destined especially for older boys and girls in displaced persons camps. The "Pieces for Peace" project of 1949 resulted in over 700,000 pounds of new materials which would give useful employment as well as new clothes to the women in refugee camps. This dramatic pointing up of the needs of women overseas brought a tremendous response, and projects of material aid in addition to gifts in money continued to be a part of every World Community Day observance.

UCCW was now, on request, represented officially at meetings of UNESCO, FAO and ECA. In co-operation with the Exchange of Persons program of the State Department, ten German women came in 1950, and church women planned contacts for them in this country. They carried out another type of activity in the "Mobilization for Peace" campaign in 1948. A million and a half commitment cards were distributed, pledging all its women signers to work and pray for peace, to seek support for the United Nations, and to help establish civil rights in their own communities. In a special ceremony Mrs. Sibley presented the signed cards to officers of the United Nations and the State Department. This ceremony and the story of the "Mobilization for Peace" campaign received considerable press publicity.

In Christian Social Relations, new projects were also undertaken with the aid of the Rosenwald Fund gift and the services of a full-time director. Four fields of work of special interest to women were set up: Family Life and Child Welfare, Race Relations, Economic and Industrial Relations, and Legislation. In 1946, only fifteen state councils had Christian Social Relations committees, but by the time of the Milwaukee Assembly in 1948 there were forty-one. A manual to encourage the work of local committees had been prepared under the challenging title, "For Souls That Greatly Dare."

Church women were concerned for the protection of children and strongly supported the new Children's Bureau of the government. In 1948 the study theme chosen for May Fellowship Day was "Every Child Is My Child." UCCW participated actively in the national conference on Family Life that same year and followed up in 1949 with the study theme, "Freedom's Foundation, the Christian Home." "Women and a Christian Economy" came next. There was the constant emphasis on social action as a responsibility of every church woman. May Fellowship Day had now become "the dramatization of the concern of the Christian lay woman in social relations in every community."

On the front page of every issue of *The Church Woman* during these years appeared a section called "Catching up on the News For and About Women," calling attention to women's achievements. UCCW rejoiced vicariously in them all. Miss Helen Kenyon, one of its leaders, was the first woman to be elected moderator of the Congregational Christian Churches; Mrs. Leslie Swain, the first woman president of the Northern Baptist Convention, was appointed a member of the powerful ninety-member Central Committee of the World Council of Churches; Dr. Mildred MacAfee Horton, president of Wellesley, became the first woman vice-president of the Federal Council of Churches; Mrs. Mary McLeod Bethune, founder of Bethune-Cookman College, was the first Negro woman to receive an honorary degree from a white college. Let all church women be encouraged by such "firsts"! But on the other hand the number of women in Congress ought to be increased. Seven was a too pitifully small number after a quarter century of suffrage!

The leadership of women had a local side as well as these lofty goals of achievement. The training of new leaders was a responsibility of every council. "How-to-do-it" aids appeared. "My Job as Chairman," for each program committee, appeared in packets. "How to lead a successful discussion" cost 15 cents. Every issue of *The Church Woman* filled its leadership page with suggestions: "Prepare in advance. Have an aim and ask if it was accomplished. Remember it is better to have six women who participate than sixty who merely listen and do nothing!" It was all part of helping women play a larger part in a new world. For too long they had been the largest unused resource of Church and community.

By 1949, Mrs. Emory Ross was made director of leadership training, and for the first time there was someone on the national staff to "help women help themselves" in training for more effective service. Another part of her assignment had to do with public relations. This department was set up in 1945 in recognition of the need to keep the public in general, and women in particular, aware of UCCW events as they occurred. In 1949, UCCW produced its first filmstrip in connection with the World Day of Prayer. It was an expensive venture, but the Council of Home Missions helped with the financing and 650 copies were immediately sold, and other filmstrips soon attempted. Radio kits for local councils were also prepared. In 1948, the Protestant Radio Commission was formed and UCCW co-operated actively as it did later in Religion in American Life. In 1949, there were twenty-one state chairmen of public relations, twenty-one film chairmen and twenty radio chairmen. The task of "bringing greater understanding of our purpose, and extending the efforts toward its fulfillment through the press and other mass media of communication" seemed well under way.

At the fourth biennial Assembly of UCCW at Milwaukee in 1948, Mrs. Worrell retired as general secretary, and Mrs. W. Murdoch MacLeod assumed that responsibility. Mrs. MacLeod's experience in the work of her own denomination, the Presbyterian Church, US, and in the YWCA, fitted her to carry it ably, and her personal qualities of courage, graciousness, and firm belief in the values of UCCW were those that were most needed during this time of decision.

In summing up the movement from the vantage point of six busy years, Mrs. Worrell touched on some principles which were already furnishing creative clues to the work of the UCCW Planning Committee on the proposed merger:

> Its [UCCW] values must be conserved, not for the sake of an organization but for the sake of the contribution it has made and will make to the building of the kingdom. . . .
>
> Its freedom from ecclesiastical control has proved to be one of its strengths.
>
> It would be a tragic loss for UCCW to have no relation to the proposed merger. But the basic structure must not be destroyed in any way. Therefore its identity must be conserved. There are several ways of merging: unity by absorption, by amalgamation or with diversity.

At the board meeting in October, 1947, an important statement was issued outlining in positive fashion the minimum provisions which, the Planning Committee felt, would be constitutionally needed to preserve the "identity" of the women's movement:

> 1. Full right to continue to organize, develop, and serve local and state councils of church women.
>
> 2. Full right to call a national assembly to review work, set goals, adopt a budget, and decide ways of securing it.
>
> 3. The right of local and state councils, either as entities or as parts of larger councils of churches, to select their own

officers and committees, raise and disburse their own money, and draw into their fellowship any Christian women willing to subscribe to and help carry out the purpose of the organization.

4. Assurance of representation on the various sections and committees of the National Council, including representation on the governing board and the executive committee.

5. The name of the women's group in the National Council, while not of prime importance, must be one giving it sufficient identity.

It was of the greatest possible help, in all the subsequent deliberations of this committee and of the larger Planning Committee of the National Council, that the women had so clear a statement of the principles which they felt must be the basis of negotiation and planning.

At the Milwaukee Assembly in 1948, there was a discussion of the question of the merger, but it was inconclusive, and the motion was carried to refer the final decision to the new national board with power to act, "after adequate study and full expression of opinion by state and local councils throughout the country." Mrs. William Sale Terrell, who was thoroughly conversant with all aspects of the question, and ideally suited for the exacting task of representing UCCW interests on the National Planning Committee, was appointed chairman of the committee to carry out this assignment.

Mrs. Terrell took the position that the task of her committee was to *inform* women's groups in the country, not to *influence* them. Under the caption "We Must Decide," a full statement of all aspects of the question of the proposed merger was prepared by the committee and printed in *The Church Woman*, March, 1949. It was admirably thoughtful and complete, free from emotional bias, and ending with these quiet but challenging words:

It is a difficult, a tremendously difficult decision to make.

The national board and our officers have spent long hours trying to think and pray it through. We are asking you to do the same, and then after careful study and sincere prayer for wisdom and guidance, to let us know your conclusions.

Though the board had been given the official power to act, it was really the church women in the country as a whole who must indicate the answer. Material for study and information was sent to every council, together with an "Opinion Poll" to register the considered opinion of the local group and be returned to headquarters. The process must be trusted fully. Was UCCW's faith in the democratic process, in women's good judgment, and in the guidance of God, strong enough to bring it through to a right decision?

There is every evidence that the local councils approached the question in the same spirit as the national committee. In the August-September issue of *The Church Woman,* Mrs. Terrell reported that replies to the Opinion Poll had been received from sixteen states and 258 local councils. More were daily coming in. Six of the eight constituting agencies and more than twenty ecclesiastical bodies had already voted affirmatively for the proposed merger. One sentence in the report, while not unduly emphasized, was noted by every woman who read it: "It is only fair to remind ourselves that in the event of a negative decision a Woman's Department will be set up within the National Council in which case UCCW might find itself outside the main stream of the co-operative ecumenical movement." It was an important point.

The board meeting that fall was to be held in Los Angeles, and the committee set about seeing how travel plans could play a part in "informing the country." The opportunity this afforded to hold seminars on all aspects of UCCW program and to ask and answer questions about the merger was too fortunate to be missed. An elaborate schedule of meetings was set up. Board members were divided into fifteen teams to cover council groups in twenty states west of the Mississippi and the general theme for the seminars would be "Women in the Ecumenical Church." Large numbers of women, many of whom had never been to an Assembly, attended and discussed what was on their minds. It was an unusual trek, but a most rewarding one. By the time the board members met in Los Angeles in October, they had a very good idea of the thinking of the country. There was, as always, a full agenda to be considered, but in the midst of it five hours were set aside for an unhurried consideration of all aspects of the merger before the final vote was taken.

Each one of the interchurch agencies had been asked to draw up suggested by-laws. Those submitted by UCCW had been carefully drawn on the basis of the principles originally stated in 1947 and incorporated some changes which made the proposed structure more acceptable. Instead of a Joint Department related to all four divisions of the new National Council (Church and Community, Christian Education, Home Missions and Foreign Missions), UCCW would become the "General Department of Church Women" co-ordinated with a General Department of Church Men (to be set up), directly related to the central administration. The new General Department of United Church Women would maintain its own existing charter for legal purposes, and the right to maintain its own department structure, including budget and business committees.

It was on the basis of these new by-laws, which had been accepted in principle by the National Committee before the Los Angeles meeting, that the vote would be taken. The major concerns of the UCCW seemed to be assured. There is no doubt that an important element in that decision was the fact that if the vote was negative, some form of Woman's Department would nevertheless be set up, implemented through the denominations. Discussions in the country had revealed unquestionably that church women felt that a general department should be the channel through which the National Council was related to organized women's work.

The position of the women was a positive, not a defensive one. They had faced all their doubts and questions. In a choice between their own organization and that of the "whole Church" they knew now what the choice must be. They really believed in the "wholeness of the Church." They must not, in the name of protecting their organizational interests, be in fact an instrument of division. Safeguarding the values that were basic to their effective functioning had now been done to the best of their corporate wisdom. To hold out for the greater freedom of action and the greater degree of inclusiveness in membership which some still felt could only be achieved by complete independence, was of lesser value than to be a part of the life of the whole. The united work of the women of the churches in the service of the kingdom must be done from now on within the larger framework of the whole. They were ready to take the step.

Mrs. LeGrand reported: "For five hours we talked, questioned, conferred and prayed. No haste. Every woman had full opportunity to ask about every word in the proposed by-laws for the integration of UCCW into the new NCC. Then in the attitude of prayer for guidance the first vote was taken and with only three dissenting votes the United Council had decided to participate in the Constituting Convention, December, 1950, of the new National Council of Churches. . . . Then all rose and without any sense of division we sang together 'Praise God from Whom All Blessings Flow.'" The year of study and consideration called for by the Milwaukee Assembly had come to completion in an overwhelmingly affirmative vote.

Women could always combine solemnity with a light touch. Someone had suggested that, in the approaching "marriage," a dowry was called for. "Of course we need to bring something with us," they said, "but not a dowry —a gift of thanksgiving for this forward step toward the realization of the ecumenical Church."

Mrs. Sibley was especially eager that women enter the new relationship, with all its possibilities for the future, not empty-handed but from a position of strength that might be a fitting symbol of women's participation. The imaginative idea of an "Ecumenical Register" suggested itself, and was launched in December of the same year. "It is a moment when Christians need to stand and be counted," she wrote to the country, "We will create a register of church women, signed with their names, addresses and denominations, with a dedication of dollars. We will make 1950 a Year of Jubilee!"

The idea was picked up with enthusiasm, and plans were laid to promote it, under the leadership of Mrs. J. Wallace Hamilton, New York, chairman, and Miss Edith Groner, associate general director. No one was to give more than one dollar, but every woman in the churches was invited to participate as a token of her interest in the ecumenical movement and women's part in it. For the next months the slogan, "Be one of the first 1,000,000 women to sign the Ecumenical Register of United Church Women!", became familiar everywhere. The goal of one million dollars was not achieved but before May, 1951, when the Register was officially closed, the very substantial amount of approximately $300,000 had come in one-dollar gifts. The fund was used to forward the ecumenical ideal, and in the next years after the merger helped to finance some of the most imaginative of the projects undertaken by the General Department of United Church Women.

The real success of the Ecumenical Register however was not measured by the dollars, but by the increasing number of women in local communities who in this way became informed about and committed to the ecumenical movement. As a public relations project in positive support of the new National Council of Churches it could hardly have been surpassed.

The impending merger did not overshadow other ongoing interests at the fifth biennial Assembly of UCCW at Cincinnati, November 13-16, 1950. Seven hotels had to be enlisted to house the hundreds of women who attended. A historical drama in costume, "This Noble Permanence," caught the mood of this last official meeting of an organization whose name was changing, but whose work and sense of purpose were continuing. The presence of Dr. Sarah Chakko, president of Isabella Thoburn College in India, and the first woman vice-president of the World Council of Churches, symbolized its link with the world Church, as did that of Dr. Samuel McCrea Cavert and Dr. Roy G. Ross, the new relationship with the National Council.

Church women were indeed entering with "strength." Even since 1948, three hundred new local councils had been added to their roster, making a total of 1,742. State councils had now been organized in every state in the Union as well as Hawaii and the District of Columbia. In terms of individuals it was not unrealistic to estimate the total membership at ten million church women.

Mrs. James D. Wyker was elected the new president. She would be known as "president of United Church Women," though she served as chairman of a General Department of NCC. Nothing in program and little in administration would change. But a new dimension and new relationships had been added. United work among church women was entering a new phase which would test the maturity of its leadership and would summon all women to participate more completely in the life of the whole Church, locally and nationally.

Two weeks later the Constituting Convention for the National Council of Churches met in Cleveland, Ohio, in an almost disruptive snowstorm. Yet many women who had been at Cincinnati were present among the 4,000 delegates who participated in the ceremony officially uniting twenty-nine denominations and eight agencies in a new inter-church enterprise, which linked 32 million church members in 150,000 churches across the land. It was a high moment. The results of it could not possibly be foretold, but the decision had been pivotal for all the church bodies involved. American Protestantism felt a new strength in facing the issues of a very troubled world, and addressing itself to problems of the Church and American society in mid-century. Women shared this, and knew in their hearts that their dream and conviction had guided them strangely, but rightly, through the valley of decision.

CHAPTER 6

"Better than a Known Way"
1951-1961

THE mood of America during the nineteen-fifties was one of anxiety. International relations with Russia were tense and uncertain and seemed to depend on the softer or harder attitude which the Russian dictatorship chose at any given moment to take toward the free world. By 1960, half the population of the world was either controlled by, obligated to, or under the influence of communistic governments. Communism was spreading not only in Asia but in South America and Africa. Countries in revolution against their status as colonies of the Western powers were particularly vulnerable.

Fear of communist infiltration gripped America and a wave of hysteria spearheaded by overzealous investigations of the Senate and House Committees on Un-American Activities, became itself a threat to democratic rights and freedoms. Yet America was prosperous, with an ever-rising standard of living and a population pushing toward 175 million, the acknowledged leader of the free world.

It was a decade when many turned to the Church and to religious practices to find a measure of security and peace of mind. Church membership in 1957 was estimated at 61 per cent of the population, revivals of the more restrained type represented by the Reverend Billy Graham attracted great numbers, and a "return to religion" seemed to be on the way. But spiritual renewal was difficult to estimate.

The issues on which the National Council of Churches spoke and the special emphases of the women's program are best understood against this background. If the program of UCW was to be relevant to the issues of the day, it must take a position in regard to the conflict with communism, American policy toward underdeveloped peoples, programs of foreign aid, the attitude of the Church toward problems of race at home, the growing influence of the laity and the need for long-range planning in the Church.

One of the early crises in the NCC came over the question of loyalty. Distinguished clergymen connected with the council, among them Bishop G. Bromley Oxnam of The Methodist Church, fell under the suspicion of Communist-hunters of the type of McCarthy, and the council itself was subjected to their "guilt-by-association" tactics. By forthright statements the National Council helped church people to see the distinction between the Christian approach to social issues, and communist theory and practice. In 1953, UCW took the initiative by issuing a carefully prepared study guide on "Loyalty and Freedom" and encouraged women's groups in churches and communities to discuss the issue. They distributed widely a red, white, and blue flyer, "A Christian Declaration of Loyalty," in which they said, in part:

Many valiant defenders of God-given freedom are being wrongfully accused . . .
We will uphold them;
We ourselves may for our beliefs face disapproval, insinuation, or slander . . .
We will stand.

Though not so immediately involved in the accusations as were some other organizations, UCW was thoroughly aroused. The study and declaration helped women think about ways of recognizing and combatting propaganda and make a distinction between harmful and creative ways of dealing with controversial subjects and situations. Throughout the decade there was a strong emphasis on responsible citizenship and what this required of Christians. This was true of the National Council as a whole. Notable conferences were held on various aspects of Christian Life and Work related to international and economic questions. The program of UCW was enriched by its part in all of these.

Though the relationship of UCW to the program of local councils was not changed when it became a part of the NCC, there was much in the work of the national office that was different because of it. Some services were combined for the sake of economy, as in the new Department of Publications and Distribution. Some were expanded in new combinations, as in publicity and communications. Much more was done together at every level because women were included on all levels of the NCC—General Board, national committees, and staff. National UCW assemblies would be held from now on once in a triennium, creating a three-year program cycle. It took time and patience to work out a smoothly operating, organically integrated organization. There would be inevitably moments of frustration, but with flexibility, good will, and intelligence there was steady progress. UCW had during this period not only the wise staff guidance of Mrs. MacLeod, the general director, but a succession of presidents who had wide experience in church affairs and were exceptionally able. Mrs. James D. Wyker, president from 1951 to 1955, was an ordained minister in the Disciples communion and had been president of the Ohio Council of Church Women. Mrs. Theodore O. Wedel, 1955-1959, a prominent Episcopal leader, had been a member of many lay commissions. Mrs. William Sale Terrell, of Connecticut, elected in 1958, at the Eighth National Assembly in Denver, had long experience in the work of the American Baptist Convention.

All were, in the deepest sense, committed to the "whole Church" and gave unstinted time and effort to the responsibilities of UCW in the new organization.

One of the far-reaching results of the merger was to bring UCW into much closer relationship with the women's work of the various denominations. It had been a weakness in the years before 1950 that this relationship, though recognized, had never been close. Denominational programs for women had also been growing in range of interest over the years and the time was overdue for a greater co-ordination of the whole sweep of organized women's work. The merger offered the natural occasion for this. At the Cincinnati Assembly prior to the setting up of the National Council, the UCW Board was ready to submit proposals that looked in this direction.

A statement of principles was adopted which laid a broad basis for the future. The aim should be a simplification of organization and services which would eliminate overlapping and reduce the demands made on local church women. There should be a concentration on getting the big jobs done together. Ventures should be limited to those on which there was agreement, utilizing the divisions of NCC for strengthening program content and achieving over-all aims. There must be recognition that denominations had a responsibility to contribute to the united program, as well as to benefit from it.

An immediate practical proposal was for a secretarial conference composed of the combined staffs of UCW and of denominational secretaries dealing with women's work which should meet once a year for three days. Its responsibility would be to co-ordinate the programs of the denominations with those of UCW. Each denominational secretarial group would appoint one person to be the co-ordinator of that denomination with respect to interpreting UCW, and would in turn act as a resource person for UCW.

The first meeting of the new secretarial conference took

place in December, 1950. It was followed regularly by others, and UCW and the denominational staffs found them even more useful than they had hoped. It was not difficult to agree in advance on program emphases and this facilitated long-range planning. Community-wide occasions, such as the observances of the World Day of Prayer, May Fellowship Day, and World Community Day, could be supported by the promotional weight of every denominational organization. Co-operation in program all along the line meant not only a saving of staff time, but opportunities to share the services of special personnel, such as guests from abroad and outstanding church leaders. Moreover, the secretarial conference supplied the occasion for getting acquainted as a professional group and the stimulus of exchanging program ideas and evaluation.

An executive secretary of the Woman's Division of Christian Service, The Methodist Church, put her analysis of all this in an article in *The Church Woman* a year later. "UCW is not *just another organization*," wrote Miss Thelma Stevens. "It is a channel through which organized church women of various denominations can work together. . . . State and local councils can no longer be looked upon as 'extras' by denominational groups in local churches. The program of the council has become a part of 'our' program and its effectiveness depends upon *us*—as organized denominational groups."

The channel did not work perfectly, of course, but it became a smoother and increasingly happier one as time went on. All women designated by their denominations to serve as members of the Assembly of the National Council* were invited to become members of the Board of Managers of UCW. At state and local levels also, there was a greater recognition of denominations as integral to the councils. Denominational support was solicited. Common

---

* Later changed to members of the General Board.

triennial themes were chosen: "Christianity and Freedom" for 1958-1961, and "The Church Ecumenical—Its Oneness, Its Mission, Its Ministries" for 1961-64. This too linked the program of the denominations and UCW together, as the various facets of the themes were spelled out in special studies, observances, and projects. The statement was often made now, in interpreting UCW, "We are the women of the denominations, working together." It became increasingly true.

The problem of race, historically such a major and thorny one in our country, entered a new phase during the fifties. The particular occasion was the decision of the Supreme Court in May, 1954, nullifying the legality of separate public schools for Negro and white students on the ground that "separate but equal" facilities in themselves constituted discrimination. The need of legal action to promote greater racial equality, however, had been growing in urgency ever since World War II, when Negro troops had fought to preserve democracy abroad. Surely a greater measure of it was needed at home for all citizens.

As we have seen, the united work of church women had operated from the beginning on the principle of racial inclusiveness. How else could "all women of the Protestant churches" work and plan together? Tradition and the fact that official national meetings were without exception interracial were so widely known as to have the effect of making integration the pattern for all councils. Women's committees on race relations were generally the strongest supporters, and often the initiators, of an annual Interracial Sunday in the community and other interracial church events. On the national board of UCW and in its committees Negro, Chinese, Japanese, and American Indian women worked together. At the board meeting in Washington, D. C., in October, 1945, when hotels refused to house the Negro members, the board scattered to homes of white and Negro, opened to all regardless of race. In 1946, one Negro board member rose in the national assembly to say that she had at first been doubtful of the sincerity of UCCW on this question, but now she wished to testify, "You have achieved brotherhood." But there was still much left to be done in 1950.

Beginning as early as 1946, in connection with setting up the new Department of Christian Social Relations, councils were asked to make definite studies of the attitudes of their own communities toward minority groups, and certain councils in addition were asked to make special studies of segregation. Among the resolutions passed in Milwaukee in 1948 was an early statement on school segregation that could scarcely have been stronger:

> UCCW has consistently stood for the elimination of the pattern of segregation in our schools as in every other area of society. We again urge church women to work toward this end.
>
> UCCW believes that discrimination and segregation are contrary to our Christian principles, and inimical to the democratic pattern. We call upon the Federal government to establish a nonsegregated, nondiscriminatory pattern in all federally administered establishments in our country and in our territories. We urge the immediate abolition of segregation and discrimination in the Armed Services.
>
> UCCW urges local councils to study the report of the President's Committee on Civil Rights: and to study conditions in their own communities in the light of the findings and recommendations of this Report.

The relation of human rights to "building for lasting peace" was clearly understood, and in the programs of Christian World Relations the point was constantly made that brotherhood and justice in the United States were inseparable from the larger problem of working for world community.

At the sixth Assembly at Atlantic City in 1952, at which President Dwight D. Eisenhower spoke, there was lively discussion of the issue of nonsegregated schools among the

2,500 delegates. The board meeting that year at Omaha had urged that UCW recognize the situation of tension that was developing and give race relations a high priority in its program for the next three years. In 1954 came the Supreme Court decision, ushering in a long period of public debate, violent reaction, and slow advance.

How did UCW, with its membership representative of a cross-section of churches North and South, proceed? Immediately following the decision UCW called a meeting in Atlanta of the presidents and the chairmen of Christian Social Relations of the seventeen southern states to outline steps that could be taken. Pronouncements were obviously no longer sufficient for the kind of help needed by local councils caught in controversy. One creative approach was to circularize among all councils a description of actual methods, procedures, and experience that had proved helpful and successful in some. A little pamphlet, "This Is How We Did It," which appeared in 1955, is an interesting record of the experiences of women in local councils in dealing with the issue of segregation in the most difficult place of all—their own community.

Workshops on methods were helpful. Between 1957 and 1959, with the aid of a special grant, forty-three Human Relations Workshops were held in different parts of the country, and in communities of varying sizes. Teams of leaders with knowledge and experience in the field, prepared the plans and helped carry them out. Workshops were not public meetings although most of them were interfaith. Council women from the surrounding area brought their problems and together sought creative ways of dealing with them. The workshops generated courage and hope in places where these were greatly needed.

The influence of the World Day of Prayer during this time of tension must not be underestimated. Every observance was a silent but inescapable symbol of "oneness" among Christian individuals. Sometimes the YWCA offered the only place where the observance could be held, and the two organizations supported each other in working interracially in the community.

Another long-time interest which emerged in a new phase during this decade had to do with employed women. The number of married as well as single women in the labor market had risen steadily since the war. National studies were referring to "womanpower" as one of the resources of the country. The churches needed to be aware of changing currents in the lives of women here and in other countries. It was time to take a serious look at the reasons why women of all ages would probably continue to work outside their homes, and to ask what were the implications of this for the program of the churches. As a joint project of UCW and the Department of the Church and Economic Life of NCC, a consultation was held in March, 1958, to which specialists in the industrial and business field, as well as homemakers and church leaders, were invited. Cynthia Wedel, co-chairman of the consultation, subsequently wrote a most useful pamphlet and study guide on "Employed Women and the Church." Its use brought the subject to the attention of councils and church groups, stimulated discussion, and in some instances eventuated in day nurseries and child-care centers. The questions raised could only be answered by men and women thinking about them together.

It was natural that in these years, with the public attention turned toward the new nations which were gaining independence and being admitted to the United Nations, Christian World Relations should focus its attention on the problem of emerging people. Themes chosen for World Community Day and for study included "Bread, Freedom and Dignity" (1957), "Exchange: Goods, Ideas, People" (1958), "Full Partners for Peace" (1959), and "Freedom to Know" (1961). A positive program of sharing was emphasized which supported national and United Nations programs of technical aid, and special offerings were taken to further special projects of self-help for women in under-developed areas.

One of the most unusual was a two-year pilot project in the South Pacific under the leadership of the Committee on Christian World Relations in co-operation with the South Pacific Commission. Fifteen thousand dollars a year was set aside for two years from the amount raised from the World Community Day observance to send an experienced worker, Miss Marjorie Stewart of England, to the Cook and Fiji Islands to "help village women help themselves" by learning how to work together on the needs in their own villages. It was an imaginative conception, one that was peculiarly appropriate for UCW. As a "pilot project" it was so successful that it was continued under Commission auspices after the two years were over.

The Denver Assembly in 1958, which highlighted this project in a colorful "South Pacific Evening," was also memorable for a special seminar on the civic responsibility of women and the role of the Church. Distinguished women guests from seventeen different countries participated, including Rajkumari Amrit Kaur, India's minister of health, once the only woman and only Christian in Nehru's cabinet, whom UCW brought to the Assembly for a major address. The seminar was planned by the Committee on Christian World Relations as part of a world-wide effort, spurred by the UN Status of Women Commission, to stimulate new interest in community development and increased participation of women in public life.

The success of the Denver seminar led to UCW's active participation in a notable seminar on these subjects the following year at Kingston, Jamaica, attended by more than a hundred women from the Caribbean area, and to more informal consultations with women's groups in Nigeria. The director of Christian World Relations continued to be an official observer at the United Nations, and to interpret to church women the rapid developments taking place among women in other countries. UCW made its own contribution to this by making the initial gift for a women's center in Ghana, and special projects in Nigeria and Chile. World Community Day funds also made possible a number of scholarships in 1961; $44,000 was set aside for the training of women leaders of other countries.

The fact that UCW could represent "all church women" led to other unexpected opportunities. In 1955, Mrs. Mac-Leod was invited to consult in Germany with chaplains and Protestant Women of the Chapel, an organization being established among the wives of service men stationed in Europe. A link with the church world which would not be denominational was needed, and a helpful "consultative" relationship with UCW was established as a result. Some years later, Mrs. MacLeod was invited to Alaska on a similar errand by the Commission on Chaplains and Armed Services Personnel, of which she is the first and only woman member. A "team" flew to Mexico in the fall of 1956 in response to an invitation from the Protestant women of Mexico, where contacts were made with groups of church women in half a dozen cities.

The Christian World Missions Committee continued to guard zealously all the missionary interests of the women over the years. As an innovation, it arranged in the spring of 1947 an "Ecumenical Tour" of the Caribbean area. Council women interested in visiting mission stations in Jamaica, Haiti, Cuba, Dominican Republic, and Puerto Rico, and meeting with church leaders in those countries, were invited to join. Twenty-six women from eight different denominations and fifteen states did so, and their experience was memorable. Such an ecumenical approach suggested a radically different way of looking at missions.

The 1950 Ecumenical Register fund made a number of special projects financially possible. The fund was scrupulously administered to forward ecumenical interests. The first grant made from it was, fittingly enough, to the World Council of Churches to help finance the continuance of the Commission on the Life and Work of Women in the Church. Mrs. MacLeod had been present at the first meeting of the Commission in 1949, and it was evident that much more needed to be done. What was women's relation to the "call to the laity" in the mission of the world Church? Were there—should there be—restrictions on women's "call"? UCW made an appropriation of $10,000 a year for three years to underwrite the work of the Commission for a three-year period. After 1955, this Commission expanded into a permanent department of WCC, "The Co-operation of Men and Women in Church and Society," and performs a valuable service. UCW itself appointed a committee on the place of women in the Church, and out of this grew the National Council's Special Committee on the Co-operation of Men and Women in Church and Society and Developments in the Field of the Laity.

The Ecumenical Register fund made it possible to bring various outstanding women who were leaders in the churches of other countries to the United States to share their experiences with church women here. It also made possible, in 1955, a remarkable round-the-world visit of an "International Fellowship Team." It was not the miles covered, but the conception back of this project and the way in which the members of local councils all over the country became identified with it that made it remarkable. Since 1927, more and more Christian women abroad had been a part of this World Day of Prayer observance and now, in 1955, it was celebrated in more than a hundred countries. The time had come to make this relationship more tangible. The object of the Fellowship Team was consultation with as many groups and individuals as possible in twelve of these countries. "The working of His power," based on studies in Ephesians, was the uniting theme.

Plans were laid with the greatest care. The team was to be international as well as interdenominational, and consisted of Mrs. Wyker, the American president; Miss Josephina Phodaca, retiring president of church women in Manila and an official of the United Church of her country; Miss Felicia Sunderlal, a graduate of Isabella Thoburn, just preparing to become director of women's work in the United Church of North India. Mrs. David D. Baker, editor of *The Church Woman*, was to be business manager and reporter. Her gift of rapid, vivid communication kept American church women in touch with the contacts made with thousands of their counterparts in twelve countries. The project climaxed that fall in the 1955 triennial Assembly at Cleveland, where a number of women from the colleges of the Orient which had so long received support from World Day of Prayer gifts, were special guests and speakers. For many who followed this adventure in Christian fellowship "on wings of prayer," the Church Universal became more than a vague religious phrase. It was solid and contemporary—a living reality in the midst of a troubled, swiftly-changing world.

But not all the work of these years was on the national or international level. UCW believed that "nothing is important until it becomes local." Large ideas like the ecumenical movement and world brotherhood must become embodied locally as all kinds of women worked together toward these ends. But local councils needed help. They needed it not only in developing programs with larger ideas and more content, but in administration. The "grass roots" nature of council work, which we have cited as its chief source of strength, could also be a source of weakness. Volunteer leadership could be poor as well as good. Too much "flexibility" could lead to the early death of a council rather than to a vigorous future. Programs could be "spotty." Study and discussion could be distressingly superficial. Enthusiasm, even hard work, by a few was not enough to insure a healthy council. Were there any standards for a "good" council? Perhaps they were impossible in such a far-flung movement, with only six national staff members, minimum travel and a limited budget. Leadership training was a phrase to invoke, but could it really be achieved?

But much was accomplished by working at local development from many angles. In 1952, the first complete manual, "Leadership for United Church Women," was published, a compendium of information covering suggested programs and good procedures. It was most useful. In 1953, a full-time director for leadership training was added to the national staff. "Designs" for training projects of various kinds were worked out for small and large groups. Money was made available for leadership caravans, seminars, and institutes within the states. UCW was in no danger of becoming "professionalized," but it could and did improve its efficiency rating.

State presidents met together annually after 1953 to discuss their problems at the time of board meetings. The experiment of holding in New York a national meeting for state chairmen of committees was tried and found so helpful that it became a regular feature of each triennium.

By 1960, the number of local councils had grown to 2,110. A network of area, state, and national conferences bound them together, culminating in a national assembly which now met every three years. A "Fellowship Fund" had been established to supplement the annual quota gifts from the states for national support. It was hoped that 20,000 women could be found who would give small annual gifts of $5.00 as a token of their interest in the ecumenical movement. Some of the older councils, like St. Louis and Buffalo, were beginning to celebrate fiftieth anniversaries, and others, like the Atlanta Council, could point with pride to special awards for community service.

But all, small and large, felt themselves a part of a strong fellowship within the churches. United work seemed, in its potential, to be "a flame of the Lord's kindling which none can extinguish."

The year 1961 would mark the twentieth anniversary of the forming of the United Council of Church Women, and the thirtieth anniversary of the organizing of a national church women's organization. UCW had proved, beyond shadow of doubt, its primary loyalty to the whole church. It was now working within rather than outside its organizational structure, contributing with increasing effectiveness to the progress of the whole.

In the perspective of this history some of the permanent characteristics of women's united work stand out clearly. One was the capacity for persistent effort in meeting human needs that had been overlooked. This was a capacity that combined imagination about people with hard work on necessary detail, often against opposition. We have noted many instances of this: women sent as missionaries in an age when only clerics could qualify; colleges established for women in the Orient; pressure for better standards in moving pictures; insistence on racial inclusiveness; status of women in Church and society. Examples could be multiplied many times. Many of the specific projects which women spearheaded became in the course of time generally approved and taken over by other agencies. This was the seal and proof of their validity.

A striking example of this, which came into its final phase in the late nineteen-fifties, was the concern of church women for the needs of migrant agricultural workers. As early as 1920, under the home missions program, women set up four centers in New Jersey, Delaware, and Maryland to give day care to the babies of the seasonal workers —Mexicans, Negroes, and others—who were employed to harvest the crops of berries, beans, and tomatoes in those states. It was not the low wages that aroused the women

so much as the neglect of the children in health and education, and the appalling conditions under which these migrants, whose labor was so essential to the national economy, were forced to live. Neither state nor community
acknowledged responsibility. A large part of the home mission share of funds from the World Day of Prayer was allocated to migrant work, and as this source of funds increased, the work was extended. Church women in states
like Texas, Virginia, and Michigan, where migrant workers
came in seasonal floods, raised in addition money to equip
child-care centers, clinics, and kindergartens, and followed
up their gifts by personal visits to the camps and volunteer
service. These projects and the publicity given by the wom-
en as they also worked on legislation gradually awakened
not only community but wider interest. A more adequate
ministry to migrants was organized under the National
Council, which by 1960 operated in camps in thirty-four
states, with five hundred permanent staff and eight thousand volunteers—students, ministers, doctors, and teachers.
In 1961, the amount allocated to this work from the World
Day of Prayer was approximately $100,000.

The Migrant Ministry made possible increased work in
the field of legislation. The formation of Governors' Committees and health and housing codes was stimulated. By
the time the fortieth anniversary of work with migrants was
celebrated in the spring of 1961, the attention of the whole
nation had been aroused. Women had spearheaded what
had become in time a general public concern.

Women had a flair for dramatizing issues and values,
which was not the least of their contributions. The yearly
observances of the World Day of Prayer for Missions, May
Fellowship Day, and World Community Day, and the special projects related to each, were such dramatizations and
they continued to attract community attention and response.
This was valuable even when not accompanied by as much
study and discussion as UCW could wish. Press and radio

were glad to co-operate in local coverage of meetings that were striking in conception and often included special community features. The subject of May Fellowship Day, 1960, "Citizenship: Free and Responsible," attracted unusual attention in an election year. "Free schools in a Free America" in 1957 brought members of local school boards to church luncheons in many towns and cities as invited guests and speakers for the first time.

Of special note in this connection was the seventy-fifth anniversary of the World Day of Prayer in February, 1961. Plans were carefully laid far ahead to make this event significant, symbolizing as it did the existence of an unbroken bond among Christian women around the world for three-quarters of a century. This year 145 areas would participate in the observance, in spite of the revolutions in which some were involved. A sense of the imperishable nature of this bond was sorely needed by many in 1961. As a result of plans, which themselves enlisted the co-operation of many thousands of individuals, 2,000 women out of eight countries came together in Prayer Fellowships in thirty-seven key centers around the world. In a common service of worship, supplemented by opportunities for fellowship and discussion, women gave expression to their deep longing for a greater measure of unity as Christians in a divided world, and their plans to move forward in this direction together. In the United States, the event had been preceded by the appearance of a little booklet, *There Came a Woman,* which pointed up the contribution which women had made and could continue to make toward these larger dimensions of the Church of Christ. Attendance at observances reached new figures, and there was an outpouring of gifts for the extension of the missionary work of the Church which it was hoped might even reach the appropriate anniversary figure of $750,000!

In 1961 came a new national administration, with President John Kennedy's plans for "moving America forward."

The space age had arrived, but old problems remained. With violence in Cuba, Africa, and Laos, the division of the world between communism and the free nations was more than ever an ominous reality abroad. At home the most serious social problem was still that of race. Sit-in strikes and freedom-riders challenged the slow pace of integration by aggressive action. Government action was firm. What did this continued tension mean for the churches—and for United Church Women?

At various moments in its history, the national organization had faced the need to speak forthrightly to a particular situation at a particular moment. The ability to do this could be quite as much of a contribution as a long-term project. An ability to perceive spiritual issues as they crested and to speak prophetically was needed if church women were to remain on the "growing edge" of the times. Something deep within them warned that they must always be pioneers in the work of the kingdom. It was an exciting, sobering, dangerous calling to be a "church woman" in this deeper, dynamic sense. Where this might lead or what emphases it might demand in their united program in any given decade could never be fully foreseen, even with long-range planning. But the capacity to "speak out" on behalf of spiritual values, as insight came, must be kept. Only courage and faith of this pioneering quality could really make United Church Women something other than "one more organization."

With the long record of their stand on race, it was appropriate for UCW to take a positive approach to new aspects of the question in 1961. The National Assembly would meet in October, for the first time in history in a southern city, Miami Beach, where interracial accommodations could now be assured. In the spotlight which "freedom riding" had turned on interracial travel, the determination of church women to let nothing hinder their traveling together to Florida from all parts of the country in all kinds of conveyances would be a testimony to their convictions that would be clearer and more impressive than words.

The Christian Social Relations Committee, in preparation for the Assembly, worked out a three-year plan for the denominations and UCW to act together "toward ending racial discrimination in church and community." This envisaged:

> Women of each participating denomination working simultaneously toward full participation of all persons regardless of race, within their own churches locally, and throughout its structure.
>
> Women of all denominations working together toward full participation of all women regardless of race in councils of church women.
>
> Women of all denominations working together to achieve full racial justice in whatever is the key area in the local community and in the state, whether housing, schools, employment, or voting.

The promotion of national workshops and community conferences would be included in such a plan, together with the observance of May Fellowship Day, 1963, and the one hundredth anniversary of the Emancipation Proclamation.

Only if UCW were fully united with the women of the denominations in such a purpose, sharing with them the initiative, the responsibility, and the difficulties involved, would such an undertaking, such a forward step, be possible. Was the plan prophetic of the dawn of a day of fuller brotherhood within the churches? Or was it just another dream of church women? UCW looked for light and guidance upon this and other emphases of the new triennium, to the decisions of the Miami Assembly.

The dream of a more effective contribution to the life and work of the whole Church was still alive in the hearts of church women after a hundred years. So was their conviction that it could best be made together. They had been led along a path they could not possibly have foreseen, and had accomplished in faith and prayer projects that had seemed at the time to be impossible. The course of their history had indeed been, under God's guidance, "better than a known way." There would be many more encounters with the God of history, such as they had corporately experienced, many more decisions requiring faith and courage. But they would follow on.

This book is presented by the officers and staff of United Church Women as the report of the triennium, 1958-1961, in recognition of the twentieth anniversary of the organization of United Church Women of the National Council of Churches, formerly known as the United Council of Church Women.

THE OFFICERS

Mrs. William Sale Terrell, *president*
Mrs. Jessie Jai McNeil, *vice-president*
Mrs. Wallace N. Streeter, *vice-president*
Mrs. Theodore F. Wallace, *vice-president*
Mrs. Stuart Sinclair, *treasurer*
Mrs. C. Newton Kidd, *recording secretary*
Mrs. Fred White, *corresponding secretary*

THE STAFF

Mrs. W. Murdoch MacLeod, *general director*
Mrs. David D. Baker, *director, Program Co-ordination and editor,* The Church Woman
Leslie S. Bidwell, *director, Public Relations*
Mrs. Fannie P. Byrd, *director of Publications and assistant editor of* The Church Woman
Eleanor French, *director, Christian Social Relations*
Mrs. Esther W. Hymer, *director, Christian World Relations*
Dorothy Nossett, *assistant to the general director of Finance and Office Administration*
Rev. Myrta P. Ross, *acting director, Christian World Missions* (since the retirement in 1960 of Mrs. James M. Evans)
Helen B. Turnbull, *director, Leadership and Field Outreach*
Rev. Mossie A. Wyker, *special representative*